TEST
...FUELED BY FAITH

The Vicki Zoradi Story

A Quadrilateral Amputee's
Inspirational Journey To Find
Love, Hope, & Joy

Quad 4 God! LLC

Homespun Treasures Publishing

ISBN#: 979-8-57-365504-8

Title: Tested by Fire...Fueled by Faith. Used with permission. Dara Linson, JWP. [ChibadofMV.com.]

Dedication

To my awesome God, Who sustains life!

To my loving husband, Mike:

Little did I know at seventeen that God would have chosen me for you and you for me. I am the one who greatly benefited from that pairing!

You make me proud to be called your wife.
You are selfless, kind, gentle,
A spiritual leader, and
A loving life-partner

To ALL my Prayer Warriors…Thank you.
Let's race to win the prize!

"I have fought the good fight, I have finished the race, I have kept the faith." 2 Timothy 4:7

My Dearest Readers and Prayer Warriors—

The moment I awoke from my induced coma, I knew without a doubt I needed to write my first book. I must've known deep in the recesses of my mind even back then that God had done a miracle in me. And I wanted the world to know it. I desire to bring God, my creator and sustainer of life, the glory HE deserves!

I recall verbalizing this 'future book' endeavor to most of my nurses and other caregivers in ICU and throughout my five hospital stays. Each of them and every family member also realized that I had a story to tell—God's Miracle Story!

Truly, though, this is my loved ones' story as much as it is mine. I am so very grateful that God gave me this chance to share "our" story with all of you. God bless you as you travel through your own life's journey with the blessings and tragedies set before you. May you all find God's love, hope, and joy.

"Race to win!"

Vicki

P.S. I enjoy hearing readers' stories of triumph through God. Or if you need an event speaker, please e-mail me at:

vickizoradi@gmail.com

DISCLAIMER AND TERMS OF USE AGREEMENT

The author, publisher, and LLC of this book have used their best efforts in writing and preparation for accuracy. The above entities make no representations or warranties concerning accuracy, applicability, fitness, actions, or completeness of its contents.

The story contained in this memoir is remembered at the best recollection of the author and is used solely for reading pleasure. The above entities disclaim any warranties (expressed or implied) for any particular purpose. They shall in no event be held liable to any party for direct, indirect, punitive, special, incidental, or other consequential damages arising directly or indirectly from any use of this material which is provided "as is" and without warranties.

The above entities are not liable for any sites and or links provided herein for accuracy, performance, effectiveness, or applicability. All sites and or links used are for the reader's informational purposes only.

This publication is not intended for any professional expertise—medical, physiological, sociological, psychological, or spiritual. Please seek professional assistance if needed.

FOREWARD:

"God chooses certain people to be His walking billboards, as it were, of His power and grace. They are carefully selected by our wise and sovereign God; they are people of whom you think, *Here's a Christ-follower whose faith has been through a fierce fire; tested, purified, and made far stronger than I can possibly imagine. I simply must hear her story; it's worth listening to and learning from!* To me, this epitomizes Vicki Zoradi. Vicki's testimony literally goes before her, for when I first met this remarkable woman, her deep loss made me say to myself, "True, as a quadriplegic, I do not have use of my arms or legs, but Vicki does not even *have* arms or legs." It makes her contentment in Christ, profound and unmistakable. It also makes her zeal to share God's abundant provision in her life so winsome. I look at Vicki, listen to her counsel, and am convinced that if Jesus Christ can sustain her, He can sustain me!"

– **Joni Eareckson Tada,** Joni and Friends International Disability Center

---

"I have been privileged to be Vicki's pastor through this ordeal. It is a joy to see her leveraging this horrific experience for the *glory of God*—as I knew she would. Vicki is genuine and sincere as she presents these words to you. I can attest that her redemptive story comes from a place of complete authenticity. I highly recommend this book and pray it will be an encouragement to everyone who reads it."

—**Pastor Mike Fabarez**—Compass Bible Church—Aliso Viejo, Ca.

PROLOGUE:

Tragedy strikes when one least expects it. The crazy thing was, I did not even see it coming—no one plans for an event like this. I was casually driving through, believing life was cruising along as it should. Year after year, seasons were racing rapidly into the next, week approaching week, sunrise to sunset. Then *WHAM*!

Infection slammed into me as if it was an eighteen-wheeler on an icy-slick expressway. It slid, swerved, smashed into, and totaled my supercharged race-car called *Life*. This unexpected, near-fatal *'crash of affliction'* barreled through my intersection with failed brakes. I could not avoid it. What chance did I have for survival? I slammed on the brakes, cranked the wheel right, prayed an instant prayer for help, and braced for impact. My idyllically, peaceful life was milliseconds away from disaster. The journey ahead was full of twists, bends, hazardous turns, road detours, flashing lights, and treacherous driving conditions. *No fear!* I put God in the driver's seat. He was the One who steered while I trusted Him to get me over the finish line safe and secure. So, buckle up and join me *(in the backseat!)* on this road of life where tragedy, trials, and turbulence turned to success, triumph, and victory!

TABLE OF CONTENTS

REFERENCE RACING FLAGS INFORMATION [1]

Green Flag = Signals a start of a race or a clear track to race on.

Yellow Flag = Caution @ 80 km/h (49.71 mph) with "safety car" for speed restrictions. No passing allowed!

Pink Flag = Drivers must slow to 60 km/h (37 mph). Do not overtake until Green Flag is waved.

Red and Yellow Vertical Striped Flag = Slippery Track Surface Ahead.

Red Flag = Suspension of the current session; proceed to pit road or STOP IMMEDIATELY.

White Flag = NASCAR's Start of the final lap.

Black and White Checkered Flag = Winner!

South Fork of the American River—Below Family Cabin

First Car—1968 Datsun Roadster 2000

CHAPTER 1

PERPLEXING PREDICAMENT

"Even though I walk through the valley of the shadow of death, I will fear no evil for you are with me; your rod and your staff they comfort me." Psalm 23:4

Catastrophe struck on my 60th birthday. Can you believe it? What are the chances? Life had been so normal. It had always been normal—a marriage of 39 years to a wonderful husband, Mike, which had produced two married children and one infant grandson. I taught second grade only three weeks prior. We were mentors in our young families' Thrive group at church. Both of us had mapped out our final stretch toward retirement. Like I said, "Extremely normal." Nothing out of the ordinary.

But, would we be prepared for this treacherous road ahead?

Yellow Caution Flag!
Flash Flash Flash - Warning Sign Posted:
Detour—Keep Right...

Mike and I were at our family's cabin in Kyburz, California, halfway between Placerville and South Lake Tahoe—as we celebrated my birthday and the Fourth of July with our daughter Tiffani and her husband, Mike Washburn. We had been at the river all day. We sat in beach chairs and enjoyed the California sun and the fresh mountain water as it splashed around our feet. I mildly suffered from a backache later in the day and attributed it to lounging awkwardly in my beach chair. Tiffani and my husband Mike switched off and rubbed my lower back on the right side. It felt better while they massaged it, but soon it became more and more troublesome as the evening progressed.

We had planned a wonderful Fourth of July dinner on the deck—barbecued chicken, corn on the cob, and watermelon, of course. Afterward, as the sun drooped behind the pines, Tiff and son-in-law Mike W asked us if we would enjoy heading to Tahoe with them to experience the city's grand fireworks display. I quickly declined. Unrelenting back pain became more prevalent in my mind with each click of the clock. They took off after they had grabbed coats and blankets to view the anticipated fire flowers over Lake Tahoe. I imagined the beautiful bursts doubled in the water's reflection. As young marrieds, both were excited to head out together. They also took the only transportation we had that week while we vacationed at our isolated river retreat.

Pain intensified.

Around 10 pm that night, Mike asked if I thought we should head to bed. For some reason, I wanted just to sit and ponder my painful predicament. *Why was I so apprehensive? Did I have an inkling of what was to come?* Mike reassured me that holiday night that he would rub my back in bed until I fell asleep. Which I did, but for a very short while. I momentarily awoke to hear the kids as they returned soon past midnight. But by 1:30 am in the wee hours of my birthday, July 5th, the pain in my back had moved to the lower right front side. This predicament frightened Mike as he voiced, "Oh no! It may be your appendix." We chose not to wake or worry the kids. Moments later, after Mike quietly locked the front door, he drove me swiftly off this Sierra Mountain to seek medical help.

Mike kept praying to God constantly on my behalf as we traversed down the curvy mountain road. We needed to make a crucial decision within the next 5-10 minutes, though. Do we keep traveling on towards Sacramento *(an additional 40 minutes, not considering holiday traffic),* where Sutter Memorial Hospital had a Trauma Center? Or, do we take a chance with the closer community hospital Marshall where I would be examined right away?

10

Mike had not received clear direction from God, so he asked me what I wanted to do. I replied, while hunched over in the front passenger seat, that my pain was pretty severe. I chose the closest hospital. Mike pulled off the highway and stopped at Marshall Hospital in El Dorado County's Placerville—a gold-rush mining town in the mid-1800s formerly known as *'Hangtown' or 'Old Dry Diggins.'* It was now after 2 am. I was thrilled at the idea that I soon would be receiving immediate, middle of the night, medical attention. I thought for sure my appendix would need to be taken out that pre-dawn morning—my birthday morning.

When I signed my name at the front desk of the emergency room, the admitting nurse noted that it was my birthday and jokingly expressed, "What a lousy way to celebrate your birthday!" "Wouldn't you know it's my 60th milestone, too," I added? We shared a silly half-baked chuckle despite my constant pain. She took my vitals then passed me off to the RN assigned to me. She gave me a gown to change into while she prepped the room. She also told us the doctor's name who was scheduled to work that shift.

After a CT Scan was read less than two hours later, the physician came in and exclaimed, "Good news! You are just passing a kidney stone. No appendix problem here. You need to go home, rest, drink lots of water, strain your urine, and see if the stone will pass." He handed Mike a prescription for pain before I got permission to get redressed.

We had a quick prayer of thanks to God after returning to the car because this was not appendicitis as we had feared. Mike and I headed back to the cabin early that July 5th morning.

But, little did we know then that I would be rushed back to the same ER within 36 hours as I fought for my life. My upcoming lineup of future experts would be needed to battle mightily for my survival!

~*~

As I rested on the love seat at the cabin, I appreciated God's outside creation during most of my birthday. This was just what my doctor had suggested. I napped, guzzled water, took my pain medication prescribed, ate a little, and took advantage of several bathroom trips throughout the day. After I had slept and felt like a lazy slug all day, I returned to light activities—reading, crocheting, and laying on a lounge chair outside on the deck.

While I prepared our salad for dinner that night, I noticed the clock on the microwave just flashed 4:22 pm—my exact birth time. It was official. *Whoa, I am now 60 years old!* A brand new decade had begun. That birthday evening, the four of us had an early celebratory meal with my favorite Scotch-a-Roo dessert. All three sang *'Happy Birthday'* to me before Tiffani cut into that oozy-gooey, most heavenly rice-crispy chocolate treats. I took in this sight and relished the love I had for each one of them while I rested in the fact that they returned my love.

Soon after dinner, I again was my jovial self. Pain medication worked—*check.* Full tummy—*check.* Chocolate fix—*check.* Since it was my birthday, Tiff and the guys cleaned up the kitchen mess. The kids then asked if I felt up for playing some card games on the deck. I agreed that I would take pleasure in whipping them both in a game of Spades and also Backgammon.

We listened to many outdoor sounds that evening—the rapids of our American River flowed just yards from our back deck, my i-pod's groovy Summer 70's music, and the constant fluid laughter produced from us all. Other than the ER visit, I loved this much desired, peaceful birthday. I had immensely enjoyed this snapshot of time with just the four of us. Even though Mike and I had forfeited many outside games to Mike W and Tiffani, a relaxed night ensued as we girls lounged on the couch. My monumental bash with more loved ones the next day would come soon enough. After many thanks for all the fun birthday festivities, Mike and I headed off to bed earlier than usual that night.

I was spent.

~*~

My Sacramento family was scheduled to celebrate my Big 60th over an afternoon the next day—Friday the 6th. Mike woke me up from a sound sleep after 9 am. He knew that I required time to get ready for our family's arrival. More food and prep time was needed for a larger crowd. But, after I strained my morning urine with no complications, no blood, or kidney stone fragments, I experienced tiredness even after a decent night's sleep of over ten hours. I dressed slowly, ate a piece of buttered toast, and swallowed my pain pills. I laid down groggily once again on the love seat as we awaited their arrival.

As my extended family began to pull into the wooded, opened-spaced parking in front of the cabin, my sister Valori carried in her beautifully decorated, homemade birthday cake dessert for me—Red, White, & Blue. Unwrapped gifts were abundant. Laughter rang, while hugs were welcomed. Where was I? I still was found curled up in a prone position on the small couch.

Unfortunately, by then, I was not up for a party, especially my own. I just stayed down on the couch and overlooked the river, while family caught up with one another. After a few hellos and birthday greetings were thrown my way, I still had not felt quite up to socializing whatsoever. The family carried on with this holiday, birthday reunion without me.

Everyone felt my disappointment and grasped my *'stone'* predicament—even though no one present in the family could relate. All congregated either on the large deck or around the vast, finely crafted dining room table made by my talented brother-in-law Paul. Both were my favorite places to gather at the cabin to share recent news with others. But not that day. They tried to let me sleep.

13

But, their whispers got louder with excitement. Talking spilled over into laughter, then laughter turned to roars. The noises they made were much like our tumbling river below. I missed it all. My sister came in for a while and joined me on the sofa. We softly shared while she rubbed my newly manicured feet. I remembered their gifts of love and empathy as they waved to me from the deck with untold looks of sympathy.

More pain medications on an empty stomach caused nausea. I had lost valuable sleep on our early morning ER visit the day before. I drank glass upon glass of water and urinated way too often with no results. I had not passed that stubborn kidney stone. I was, needless to say, exhausted! I had never experienced a kidney stone, so I had not been granted the knowledge of what to expect. I figured what people—jokingly from a few males—had informed me before must be true, "Passing a kidney stone is worse than childbirth!"

~*~

The evening of the 6th after the family had left the cabin, Tiff and I settled in on the couch to watch our evening DVD movie, *"Monster-in-Law"* starring Jane Fonda and Jennifer Lopez [1]. I had stopped taking the prescribed pain medication earlier due to nausea—opting for Extra-Strength Tylenol® instead. I had utilized a strainer throughout the day to collect any stones that should have passed. They STILL hadn't, not one. Mike helped me as I walked to the bathroom just for safety purposes. My urine continued to be crystal clear with no blood. Zero signs of trauma. Even though sleepy, the Tylenol® had worked its magic for the pain.

As the movie began, Mike asked me a question of which I had not answered. He got very concerned and voiced this with a command, "Answer me, or I will need to take you back to the hospital!" I looked at him a little disoriented but responded nonchalantly with, "Honey, I'm just passing a kidney stone." I had not tracked what he asked of me very well, so Mike asked Tiffani what she thought.

14

Tiff turned to me and requested, "Mama, look at me..." She peered at my glassy eyes and wanted me to respond to her as well. When I didn't, she asked with concern, "Dad, have you ever seen Mom act or respond like this to you before?" "No, never..." Mike then called Mike W over from the dining room table as he wrote his term paper. All of them unanimously agreed.

Something was wrong. *Terribly wrong!*

~*~

We piled into the Highlander around 9 pm. All three rushed me back ASAP to Marshall Hospital. This leg of our trip became life-changing for all of us. Just moments before, I had walked out to our car unassisted. All along the first ten or so minutes on our drive, they recalled and noted in their iPhones™ which medications I had taken over these last few days, in case I should have a different physician upon re-examination. I was cognitive enough and added a med that they had forgotten to their list. All three thought at the time that I was just having some simple reaction to my prescribed medications. I was a novice regarding any pharmaceuticals.

Mike pulled the car into the closest parking lot and raced up to the hospital's front curb. After Tiff had commandeered a wheelchair for me at the curbside drop-off, she and my concerned husband rushed me in through the same automatic double doors while Mike W *"Uncle Dubs"* parked the car. The nurse immediately recognized me and quickly took my vitals. She shared out my extremely low blood pressure to my family—"65/35." Since Mike ran a healthcare training company—Medcom, Inc.—and had been in the healthcare industry for the last forty years, he knew that my blood pressure was extremely low. So this nurse's revelation worried them all even more.

That was all I remembered. I was out cold.

Within seconds, the emergency room doctor joined five or six nurses who assisted him on my behalf. Two put IVs in both my arms and proceeded with fluid resuscitation. They attempted immediately to bring about a rise in my blood pressure. I had all the classic signs that pointed to **septic shock**— serious blood poisoning! A major infection had spewed throughout my entire body. I was out of it, comatose, unaware of what had happened to me or what was about to occur further along this road of infectious disease.

Thank you, God. He had made sure the trip from the cabin started a few nights ago at this particular, reputable, community hospital. Their staff already had my computerized file, kidney stone information, and previous CT Scan results. God had taken the wheel. My survival would be determined by God and their quick medical attention. Even with speed in my favor, recovery during this final stage of sepsis was a long shot. Treatment needed to occur pronto. We had just completed the 31-mile trek from Kyburz to Placerville which took a minimum of half an hour. Each moment in this type of crisis was deemed precious. Every second made the difference between life or death.

I would not have survived the extra 42.4 miles further to Sacramento. The doctor informed Mike that I would surely have died, no doubt, if we had headed to Sutter Memorial's Trauma Center the previous night. If I had gone there in the first place 30-plus hours before, specialists on my case were confident I would not have survived.

To die on a crowded freeway in my own car on my celebratory birthday/holiday week was inconceivable. Just think...I would have passed away unaware that my precious husband and loving kids would be destined to endure that horrific memory. A lifetime flashback of personal trauma, as they held my limp, lifeless hand while I breathed my last breath. They would be forced to watch me as my life slowly slipped away from theirs on a long, lonely highway.

~*~

All of my organs started having difficulty even on that short stretch of two-lane, mountainous highway. They had already been in major jeopardy of shutting down completely by 10 pm that fateful night. The kidney stone had been blocked completely in the ureter. This stone traffic jam flushed and forced toxic urine back up into my right kidney which quickly turned into an all-out, full-body, E.Coli infection.

Within seconds after we had arrived in the ER room, my family's hope for my survival was barely dangling by a string—just like the used, pine-smelling, tree-shaped air freshener I had hung on my rearview mirror. During this race against time, each one of them was too stunned and paralyzed with fear to form rational thoughts. They—like me—were unaware that my zooming car was destined for an imminent *'crash'* due to a major illness. An illness that eventually caused me permanent body damage.

Hope was put on hold. My loved ones, who eye-witnessed sepsis viciously as it raced through my veins, felt frozen on this ER racetrack. They had not quite understood the seriousness of my medical issue. Worried, concerned, and troubled described their demeanor as they watched medical personnel in action. These medical 'Road Warriors' purposefully and determinedly dashed around me like cars on a racetrack. As this new medical trauma unfolded, Mike and my two children were left wide-eyed and baffled...

Just an hour ago, Mom had walked, talked, and ate with us. How could this be happening to her?

Mike, Tiffani, and Mike W were in total shock.

Surreal. This must be a nightmare! Poor Mom...This can't be happening right now!

Kidneys are the second largest organ to push cleansed blood throughout the body. My E.Coli-infected kidneys blasted the infection throughout my entire circulatory system. The ER doctor ordered those two IVs stat within seconds as they got my limp body onto the gurney. The staff had worked frantically around my bed as all tried their best to get me stabilized, but with each tiny movement, my blood pressure and pulse plummeted even lower.

"50/35!" a nurse informed the attending physician. My blood pressure got so dangerously low that death was thought imminent. That's when Mike questioned the doctor in charge, "What is happening to Vicki?" From my Emergency Room's doorway, my anxious husband Mike and distressed daughter Tiffani—both with rounded eyes—had intently watched with confusion all the commotion around me. The physician in charge answered Mike on the spot...

"Your wife's condition is life-threatening!"

"Life-threatening? Right now?"

"RIGHT NOW!"

Red Flag warning...Driver's suspension

~*~

I desire the severity of my condition realized at that moment. I found the following *Mayo Clinic* definition of **Septic Shock** helpful:

"...a widespread infection causing organ failure and dangerously low blood pressure. Septic Shock is a life-threatening condition caused by a severe localized or system-wide infection that requires immediate medical attention. Septic shock has a greater risk of mortality than sepsis alone. It is rare. There are less than 200,000 U.S. cases per year. Symptoms include: low blood pressure, pale and cool arms and legs, chills, difficulty breathing, and decreased urine output. Mental confusion and disorientation may also develop quickly." [2]

I had ALL these symptoms.

"*Treatment consists of fluids and blood pressure support. Emergency treatment may include supplemental oxygen, intravenous fluids, antibiotics, and other medications.*" [2]

Yes, ALL those treatments as well. I was in serious trouble without even realizing it. *Healthline.com* posted that same summer,

"*There are three stages of sepsis: sepsis, severe sepsis, and septic shock. Diagnosis is often made with a blood test. This type of test can determine if any of the following factors are present:*

*Bacteria in the blood.

*Problems with clotting due to low platelet count.

*Excess waste products in the blood.

*Abnormal liver or kidney function.

*Decreased amount of oxygen.

*Electrolyte imbalance." [3]

I had every one of these conditions. This was the first warning sign that several dangerous obstacles and detours were ahead on my route.

~*~

I had never been sick other than just typical flu bugs or colds. Once I had salmonella poisoning and another instance the H1N1-swine flu. But with antibiotics, I had bounced back quickly. I had over 100 sick days that remained on my personnel account at my school district. Fifteen days earlier, I had just successfully completed my 21st year as an elementary school teacher. I taught another highly challenging year of 2nd grade. I experienced that most difficult school year with its varied readers leveled from Kindergarten to sixth grade and all readers in between. Some students were dyslexic, anxious, behaviorally challenged, emotionally charged, or experienced scotopic sensitivity while reading. Yet, I strove with high determination to help encourage each one. I took command and ownership as a fiercely driven competitor, but with much gentleness and self-control as possible.

Self Determination...

So for Mike or Tiffani to see me in this weakened state was, needless to say, quite literally *ALARMING*! This was only the beginning of many uphill climbs to regain my health and strength. My *"race car"* for the next few months spun out of control. Out the window went my neatly packaged, beautifully wrapped, tied up with a frivolous bow "Life."

S-T-O-P!

Immediately, a concealed *'Stop Light'* had come into view. It had abruptly turned from yellow to RED. I slammed heavily on my brakes with both feet—*FULL FORCE.* At this high speed, I began to fishtail. It was obvious that I was no longer in control. This ride of mine headed straight into a disastrous pile-up. I could do nothing to correct my fate. It was impossible to STOP in time. I skidded through the intersection where a *'Semi-Truck full of Infection'* and my Roadster collided. It had crushed and totaled my machine's body and performance.

What now, God?

- God is Sovereign.

- God is The Mastermind Maker of all.

- God is my Great Physician.

- God had been for quite some time and always will be my Dedicated, Designated Driver of this automobile.

I have a deep love for God. I had known for many years that God is in control of everything. I had put my trust in Him. And I am just along for the ride. In this particular NASCAR race with infection, my totaled race car was towed off the track. I switched car **and** driver. I found myself unable to complete even one more lap. Yellow flag automatically replaced with a solid RED FLAG. I was dragged into the pit crew's stop area in an emergency. I no longer cared if I forfeited my own points, stats, or purse money [4]. I needed a new car and driver pronto to complete this race.

I had found myself passed out in the back seat. But during this ICU Interstate's service stop, my God had me safely protected in His mighty hands. My Heavenly Chauffeur gripped the steering wheel firmly confident—And took off! Back on our race together. My Driver had maneuvered my life right on the path He wanted me to go.

Green flag back up...Jesus once again raced His
unconscious companion on towards the finish line...

Let's continue to drive along this crooked path through adversity to view—through revealed prayer requests and conversations—the dire needs that immediately faced my loved ones and me that summer. God's amazing healing power and His answered prayers were fully on display in a timeline that's difficult to believe. Believe it. Because it happened to me...

BUT GOD...

"I believe that I should look upon the goodness of the LORD in the land of the living! Wait for the LORD; be strong, and let your heart take courage; wait for the LORD!" Psalm 27:13-14

"But you, O GOD my Lord, deal on my behalf for your name's sake; because your steadfast love is good, deliver me!" Psalms 109:23

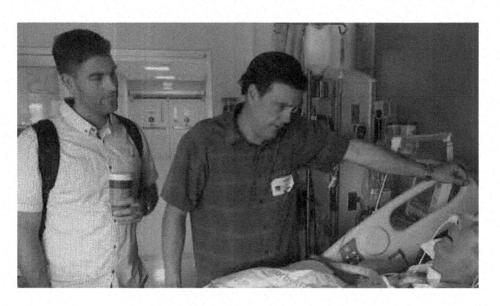

MARSHALL HOSPITAL
BEFORE 'MIRACLE TUESDAY'

CHAPTER 2

POWER OF PRAYER

"Answer me when I call, O God of my righteousness! You have given me relief when I was in distress. Be gracious to me and hear my prayer!" Psalm 4:1

"For the eyes of the Lord are on the righteous and his ears are open to their prayer." 1Peter 3:12

Total shock. *Stunned.*

After my husband Mike heard this incomprehensible, devastating news that his helpmate was on death's door, Mike knew that I needed Divine help. *And Quick!* Only through God's mercy and interventions would I be healthy again. He instantly stepped out of the emergency room's doorway while he uttered a desperate prayer, *"Please God, spare Vicki's life."* Mike's second thought—*The ONLY way Vicki will survive is through the prayers of other Christian believers.* So, he and Tiff stepped back into the lobby, joined Mike W, and they texted and called others to pray in earnest for me, for us immediately.

All three soon realized that prayer was the **only** way that I would survive this devastating health trial. Their wife or mother was dying from Septic Shock—a severe infection that countless others had previously died. We had never heard before that this destructive infection had happened to anyone else we knew.

SEPTIC SHOCK—What is that? We had never even heard the term.

The first calls made were to our family members—local and out-of-town. After they heard this inconceivable news, my brother Mike and his wife

Brenda jumped in their car and began the nine-hour trip north on I-15 to I-395 to Hwy 50 from Fallbrook, California. My sister Valori and her husband Paul lived locally and had just said their fair-wells only hours before at the cabin. *How can this be true?* They came as soon as they could. Dad came the following morning.

My son David, his wife Keana, and 9-month-old Jet were finally reached early morning on the 7th and speedily were on their way from Vancouver, Washington. Unprepared, it's most difficult when a family must pack necessities for an infant while they knowingly needed to leave as soon as possible. Tiffani had told David and Keana, "Mom is in a life-threatening situation. Come as soon as you guys can!" They showed up 631 miles later.

Those with me also notified Mike's sister, two brothers, and their wives, and our best couple friends. Each was called for immediate prayers. All of them, in turn, sought prayers from all their family members, friends, and churches. Like the 1980's commercial which featured FABERGE ORGANICS SHAMPOO with Heather Locklear & Christopher Mayer..."*And so on...and so on...and so on...*" [1] Flash notifications ever widened with regards to my situation. News spread in concentric circles as much as water dripped and pooled under a hot, steamy radiator.

It was now just after 2 am, but Mike didn't care that he woke people up at the church for immediate prayer and to get prayer chains activated. He got through to our church's Home Fellowship Group leaders, who happened to be awake in a Palm Springs resort. Their air conditioner unit had quit. At 103°, after the midnight hour, they switched rooms. Jeanette conveyed to us later that her husband Mark *never* answered his phone throughout the night. But this time was different. I needed prayer! They put out a prayer request to our Bible study group and the main prayer chain at our Southern California Compass Bible Church in Aliso Viejo. [2]

Many people had begun to pray—The Prayer of Faith.

"Is anyone among you suffering? Let him pray. Is anyone cheerful? Let him sing praise. Is any among you sick? Let him call for the elders of the church, and let them pray over him, anointing him with oil in the name of the Lord...The prayer of a righteous person has great power as it is working." James 5:13, 16-17.

Mike also contacted our Thrive group leaders at church so that the Thrive Prayer Chain could be initiated. My long-time teacher friend at my school site—Lake Forest Elementary School in Saddleback Valley Unified School District—was sent a text from Mike to spread the word at school. Tiffani contacted her mentor Jenni through text messages.

The request to God to spare my life had spread out fast and sure—like exhaust that had escaped from the tailpipe. The call for prayer was sent out daily to these critical people. Family members had shown up quickly at Marshall Hospital. Others were in constant phone call communication with Mike, Tiffani, or Mike Washburn. These three were my advocates, information soldiers, and prayer heroes. They stuck with me around the clock for these first few critical hours, which turned to days, weeks, and finally months.

The tear-filled July 7th morning and all through the early dawn of July 8th continued to be an emotional, heart-wrenching, tragic reunion for family members present. Others received communications that were intimate phone calls, and these were unrecorded.

The following **actual** texts and e-mails were sent or received by Mike or Tiffani. Additional messages blasted out by pastors, leaders, Home Fellowship Group, church participants, teachers, and friends known as **My Prayer Warriors!**

Warning! Entering Perilous Path on the route.
Slow traffic up ahead.
Proceed with Caution...

Are you still buckled up?

~*~

*(The following is one month of **unedited** writers' prayers, praying out a scripture, CAPS, words, except "quoted scriptures," allowing them for emphasis and raw emotions...)* [3]

JULY

July 7th @ 9 AM *(Saturday)* "Her heart is struggling. But she is battling. Tough turn recently. Please pray."...Mike

July 7th @ 3:43 pm

Subject: EMERGENCY PRAYING! Hello small group family...

Would you please lift up Vicki to our LORD. She and Mike are up at their cottage. Vicki was treated for a kidney stone yesterday. Today she was lethargic, so they took her to the hospital. Blood pressure dangerously low. She has sepsis and the next few hours are critical. They put a stent in her ureter to bypass this stone. She is on heavy antibiotics to fight this very serious infection. Please be lifting Mike and Vicki up to our mighty LORD. Son-in-law and their daughter Tiffani are with Mike and Vicki. We will keep you posted as he lets us know.

Lord, I love you, my strength. The LORD is my ROCK, my FORTRESS and Vicki's DELIVERER. YOU are the GOD we take refuge in. You are the POWER of Vicki's salvation. YOU are her Shield and her STRONGHOLD. Psalm 18:1&2

"Have I not commanded you? Be strong and courageous. Do not be frightened, and do not be dismayed, for the LORD is with you wherever you go." Joshua 1:9

"HE alone is my rock and my salvation, my fortress; I shall not be greatly shaken." Psalm 62:2

26

Be merciful to me, O God, be merciful to me (Mike and Vicki), for in you my soul (their souls) takes refuge; in the shadow of your wings, I (they) will take refuge, till the storms of destruction pass by. A prayer from Psalms 57:1

We are praising YOU LORD for your help, strength and faithfulness during this time for them both. May you receive much Glory! Please guide the doctors with much wisdom. Please hold Vicki in your hand. Please carry Mike, Tiffani, and Mike's hearts right now.

Thank you family, Mark and Jeanette

[The following embedded are the actual phone texts *Tiffani* and her Spiritual Mentor—and my friend—*Jenni Cuccia* shared from 7/7 through 7/12 *(used with permission.) Unedited for raw emotion]*

7/7/18

Tiff—Hi Jenni. I have a huge prayer request. My mom is in septic shock right now in the ICU and she could die- it's an hour to hour thing. Pray for God to heal her please. Love you

Jenni—Ohhh my .....PRAYING NOW!!!! Is she on the Compass prayer team? Huntington Beach and Aliso Viejo?

T—She's at AV in thrive ministry. We are in Northern California. We were on vacation for her 60th Bday when this happened. We trust God will bring glory to himself thru this very hard time. It's so sad seeing my dad like this though and her fighting to just breath on her own.

J—Oh Tiffani....Can you Call the prayer team for HB and AV. I'll give you the number to AV.

T—okay yes

J—I'm getting the number for you now....."You keep him in perfect peace whose mind is stayed on you, because he trusts in you. Trust in the LORD forever, for the LORD GOD is an everlasting rock." Isaiah 26:3-4...Here's the prayer team contact!

T—thank you Jenni! I texted her.

J—what hospital. The prayer team is texting the pastors.

7/7 *later that day*

J—how's your mama?

T—It's Marshall's hospital in Placerville, CA. She is the same. Vitals are very low. On a ventilator and meds for blood pressure.

J—Oh sweet Tiffani. Praying without ceasing!

T—thank you Jenni. It's heart breaking she can't get relief of pain right now cause her blood pressure is too low for pain medicine

J—Oh Tiff. I'm sharing this with Angela. She sees a lot of serious patients like mom. She asked What kind of infection started it do you know? "He alone is my rock and my salvation, my fortress; I shall not be greatly shaken." Psalm 62:2...May I update the AV prayer for her pain and bp concerns?

T—It was a kidney stone blockage then a bacterial infection up into her kidneys which is now sepsis. She isn't breathing on her own.

July 8 @ 11 AM *(Sunday)*

Vicki is being transported to a hospital that is 30 minutes away that does continuous dialysis which can more effectively cleanse her infection. Pray that the transport goes well and she handles it well. Mike

July 8 @ 10:11 PM

subject Re: Compass prayer team update/Zoradi

Just talked to Mike and it appears there has been a slight improvement with the dialysis. Mike said the family had a worship session in the lobby and when they went back in, Vicki improved. Brain, kidneys are strong. Liver is slightly compromised. She had some stress on the heart. She has shown amazing grace through this. Her kids and spouses and brother and sister are with her. She is not in pain only discomfort from the tubes in her throat. She is fully aware and doing sign language with them! Keep praying,

Mark and Jeanette

July 8th. Compass prayer chain…

Tiffani says that Vicki is a woman who loves the Lord and desires to live her life to glorify God. Tiffani and her family want God's will to be done, but they ask for prayer for God to heal Vicki if He will. This would allow them to have more time with her and allow her to have more time to serve Christ and his church. Above all, they want to glorify Christ through this very difficult trial. They are also grateful for our prayers.

7/8/18

Jenni—Praying for your mommy and all of you this morning my precious Tiffani!

How are things going??

Tiffani—Hi Jenni...Thank you so much for your praying. My mom is not taking steps forward at this point. They are going to airlift her or take an ambulance (not sure yet which one) to a facility that does continual dialysis

J—I'm praying without stopping!! "And those who know your name put their trust in you, for you, O LORD, have not forsaken those who seek you." Psalm 9:10

T—It isn't bad news when God is in control

J—It isn't bad news when God is in control

T—Meditating this hour on Romans 8. My mom is responding when we read scripture to her.

7/8 *later that night...*

J—Praying for you precious momma. All of You are so on my heart. I love you dear one. Keep your eyes on Jesus.

T—The Lord is so with us, Jenni. We have been praying non stop around the clock. We are praying scripture and definitely not giving up hope in Jesus

7/9/2018 (Monday)

J—My precious Tiffani. How is momma. Any updates. How may we pray for you all? I love you dearly and your whole family!

T—Sweet mama is about to meet Jesus, Jenni. We had more time with reading and talking with her. We said our goodbyes and that will continue for awhile

J—Oh my Tiffani...we just prayed for you all. I'm so incredibly sorry. I love you and will keep praying. Praising God for our Jesus. Your goodbye is only I'll see you again my momma.

T—Ya I had the best time spending time going over memories, praying, and telling her how much I love her and the ways she has shaped me as a woman.

J—Your mom has been an amazing mom and you're an amazing woman because of her. She's the one that wanted you to reach out to me for Partners. I'm so grateful.

July 9th...@ 8:04pm

Compass prayer line update/Zoradi

Dear team,

Vicki Zoradi (who is in septic shock) was moved yesterday to a larger hospital where she can get continuous dialysis. Today she is not doing well. Her doctors don't think she will make it. (pH levels to sustain life needs to be over 7, but hers is at 6.75) She is surrounded by her family and they have all been reading to her and talking to her. Today Vicki's family members said their goodbyes, just in case. Vicki is in a sedated state to protect her vital organs, but doctors have said that she can probably hear her family. Vicki's daughter Tiffani says that the gospel has been talked about all day in the hospital... They have had many opportunities to share with those around them. Please pray for medical staff to respond in repentance and faith. And please Pray for Vicki as she continues this battle, and for Vicki's family.

~*~

Straight after the transport to Sacramento, an ICU vascular trauma surgeon quickly needed to go in through my main groin femur artery with a surgical procedure to find my blood pressure and pulse. He STILL was not able to find a reading for either one. ICU personnel realized as soon as I had arrived that I still hung on to life by a thread due to my flushed skin-color. Another vascular surgeon came on the scene to replace the previous surgeon. He was confident that he would be able to find it through my groin area. He was unsuccessful as well.

An ER physician told Mike some shocking information. Statistics proved a high mortality rate from septic shock with many complications and roadblocks along the way. Once I had been transferred from Marshall to Sutter's trauma ward, one of my ICU physicians confirmed with Mike, "You realize that your wife Vicki is very, very, Very, VERY ILL! ...RIGHT?" Mike tracked. He understood the severity. *Everyone* involved knew the seriousness of my predicament.

BUT GOD...

July 10 @ 12:03pm *(Tuesday)*

Hello faithful Prayer warriors, Early this morning Mike called with another update. It was a joyful/energized Mike. Yesterday, they all said their goodbyes and SURRENDERED Vicki to the LORD. He said they went into the waiting room next to her ICU room. It's the private room for them to pray, rest and sing hymns. Praising God for providing that. They sang for hours and then went to bed. They woke up to changes.

Vicki's blood pressure is now 107/79. Her lactic acid levels went down from 19 to 11. She has tremendous edema. Purple limbs and hands. Swollen. But her toenails are much better today, looking normal.

Please pray that her blood pressure will normalize on her own. She is on five meds (vasopressors) for the BP that are poisoning her. They're trying to wean her off of them. Please pray that lactic acid levels will keep dropping. They need to be at one. Due to the limited blood flow to her limbs, her hands are two times the size. They believe she may have to have all of the tips of her fingers removed. Please pray the LORD could do a mighty work even with that. She is still very sick. But God is hearing your prayers. Please continue to pray for Mike and all the 10 people of family around them. Mark will be arriving there today. He had to make these arrangements and meetings months ago. He's heading to the hospital as soon as he lands. Praising GOD for all he's done and will do. Trusting in HIM and HIS perfect will. Mike has been telling Vicki all about your love and prayers. She is aware. She can hear.

Love you all,

Jeanette

Psalm 62:2 "He alone is my rock and my salvation, my fortress; I shall not be greatly shaken."

7/10/2018

J—Sweet precious Tiffani. Praying for you all. Praying for a miracle with your mommy. I love you dearly sweet one. Angela says that momma is doing a little better and not worse...praising God.

Psalm 3:4 "I cried aloud to the LORD, and He answered me from His holy hill. Selah"

Oh Lord hear our cry!!!

T—Yes amen! We are continuing to walk this with patience, trust, and total peace with God's perfect will for my mom's life. We know she will be with Jesus one day, we just don't know if it's soon

J—I love you and am on my knees praying with an urgent heart.

T—So many people are praying. It's so encouraging. My family and I are getting so many text messages. The body of Christ really unites as one. My dad's good friend Mark O'Connor flew out to come today.

J—Wow!! My whole body just got chills!!!! We beg you Lord. Show Your GLORY IN JESUS HOLY NAME

T—Only God's children are showing up!

J—Praying with such an urgent heart my sweet Tiffani! Any updates this afternoon? Trusting in JESUS our LIVING HOPE!!! Praying for you all as well

T—He is our living hope that's right! I was reading today in John about Lazarus being raised from the dead and reading that with my mom. Asking God to basically raise my mom from the dead (even though she hasn't passed)

J—Yes!! And HE IS ABLE

33

T— I miss her terribly

J— I can only imagine how much you miss her sweet Tiffani. If you are able to talk let me know. I will call you.

July 10 @ 6:16 PM

I got to spend several hours with Mike and family and some time with Vicki today. Mike and I went to lunch away from the hospital. It was the first time away since this ordeal began. It was a sweet time. He is being an amazing leader for his family and witness to so many in the hospital. No surprise right!

Not much change with Vicki today. Her Blood pressure is holding around 100/65 or so—that's encouraging. They are trying to work her off the blood pressure meds especially the one that robs blood flow from her extremities. Her fingers and nose are blue like if she had frostbite. Her lactic acid count is around 12 versus 19. Normal is probably around one. Pray that they will be successful in moving her off the blood pressure meds. Also that they can identify the specific infection and treatment. She is still very fragile but they are optimistic. I plan on returning back tomorrow night after visiting dealers. I got to pray over her with Mike and Tiffani. Mike is so thankful for all your prayers.

Mark O.

July 11 @ 8:29 AM *(Wednesday)*

Update from Mike this morning. God is hearing prayers. Her blood pressure is getting stronger. They have successfully removed two blood pressure meds and her body is stabilizing without them. Praise. The one blood pressure med they removed was the one that caused the blue in her extremities, so another praise those areas are beginning to change. Her pH levels have normalized, praise. Didn't hear about the lactic acid level yet, but with these current changes, they are not worried. Praise. ICU doctor stated this is a miracle and has not witnessed this in the 30 years of practice. Praise. Mark will be back with Mike later today after his meetings. Sweet Vicki is not out of the woods. But all doctors are very encouraged by what they are witnessing in the last 24 hours. Please keep praying. Praise you LORD with your precious provisions, faithfulness and revealing your glory to that Sacramento hospital, doctors, nurses and to all of us. We are praising YOU LORD, all the glory. Your will be done.

Jeanette

7/11/2018

J—precious Tiffani. How is mommy this morning?!! Praying non-stop!!!

T—She is doing good! Just praying to save her hands!!

J—Oh Tiffani. Amazing. Praying for her hands. Is it to bring back her hands circulation? Praying for her hands to come back perfectly!!

July 11 @ 10:36 PM

Hello to you all who have been faithfully praying. Lifting up many praises to the Lord. His faithfulness, grace and mercy have been overwhelming. Mark spent the afternoon with Mike and family. Here is the latest update...

O2 levels given began at 90%, 80% and now they're at 50%. So she is breathing more on her own. Praise. She received a nutritional feeding tube today. Praise. They are slowly removing the excess fluids. She had 50 pounds of extra fluid, now only 35. Praise. With less edema, daughter Tiffani (occupational therapist) can rub and massage her fingers and extremities to increase circulation. Praise. Her color is improving. Only on two of the five blood pressure meds. Since she's off one particular, the frostbite, bluish color on feet, nose and hands should diminish. Praise. They identified it was a bladder infection that went to the kidneys. Because of kidney stone, a blockage occurred. Praise they found the source. The goal is to slowly remove all support and allow her body to take over. They will slowly remove meds that keep her sedated. Please pray that Vicki will be calm when she awakes. She has been through a great deal and it may be a difficult transition. Pray that they can manage any pain. Please pray for wisdom for these doctors. They have never had a patient go through what

Vicki has and now be at this stage. They are not sure what to expect. They know it will be a slow recovery. Told Mike they want her there for another four weeks. Mike wants to bring her back to Orange County as soon as she is stronger. Please keep praying for God's will. Pray for extremities to return to normal color and no nerve trauma in these areas. Pray for this new transition as they begin to remove particular medications, life-support, fluids, dialysis and oxygen. They will do this one step at a time as they feel she is ready. Please pray for God to continue to receive much glory in this situation. Please pray for many more opportunities to share the gospel. Hospital staff recognizes how precious and different this family is. Thank you Lord. Please pray for wisdom, strength, and much grace for Mike as he will have many decisions to make...

Jeanette

7/12/2018 (Thursday)

J—"I will give thanks to the LORD with my whole heart; I will recount all of your wonderful deeds. I will be glad and exult in you; I will sing praise to your name, O Most High." Psalm 9:1-2

Thanking God this morning sweet Tiffani that your momma is showing improvement! Singing praises to his NAME!!!

T—Her hands are looking a bit better!! Been reading in Luke 18 about the persistent widow this morning and been in the Psalms singing praises to my precious and holy Lord! I can't wait to see her wake up!

J—Oh Tiffani!! So praising God!! Today is the day they will try to wake her up right?

T—They tried and her breathing was not what they wanted to see. So they are just taking it off slowly. I may ask Angela about that cause I don't understand how you wean someone off of sedation meds. Thank you for the scripture, any scripture you have during this time is what I need as well.

J—"Ah, Lord GOD! It is you who have made the heavens and the earth by your great power and by your outstretched arm! NOTHING is too hard for you."- Jeremiah 32:17

"The LORD is my portion," says my soul, "therefore I will hope in him. The LORD is good to those who wait for him, to the soul who seeks him. It is good that one should wait quietly for the salvation of the LORD." Lamentations 3:24-26

"For I will restore health to you, and your wounds I will heal, declares the LORD,..." Jeremiah 30:17

T—Amen! Such great verses to meditate on! The Lord is definitely my portion!! He fills me and gives me and my family exactly what we've needed even in times of "bad news". The faith that this has continued to stir in me is only an act of the Holy Spirit dwelling in me and guiding me.

J—Any updates Tiffani? I told Ang you had questions. She's driving home now so I'm sure she will reach out when she can. Praying with urgency!!!

T—Hey sorry Jenni! She is slowly doing better, praise the Lord. They changed her sedation medicine so that when she wakes up it will make her less anxious and relieve the pain a little more. I saw her grimace her face and gag when they moved her tubes today and that was scary and made me feel bad cause it looked like she was really uncomfortable and choking. But they think she is going to wake up within a week. If everything progresses how it's been. Her hands look better as well!!! I'm seeing God do a miracle! My dad and other family members talked and shared the gospel and hearts are softening. We were saying how much we have seen God in all this. They believe but haven't trusted or repented.

J—That's a huge PRAISE!! Oh Tiffani I am praying. And so so so many....I'll be praying for her pain and discomfort to be down. And her breathing to be SO GOOD quickly!!!! Praying all glory to God through all this!! Wow. Praying for you.

T—Thank you Jenni! You've been such a faithful sister in Christ to me during this time. I am amazed at our Lord and ALL He is doing. He deserves ALL the praise and glory for everything!

J—Praying for you. This is so much for you!! May God's grace be sufficient!! "But he said to me, 'My grace is sufficient for you, for my power is made perfect in weakness.' Therefore I will boast all the more gladly of my weaknesses, so that the power of Christ may rest upon me. For the sake of Christ, then, I am content with weaknesses, insults, hardships, persecutions, and calamities. For when I am weak, then I am strong." 2 Corinthians 12:9-10

T— Yesss. I thought of these verses on day two of this trial. I also was meditating in James 1 today and the Spirit allowed me to see it so differently cause I'm actually living it! The testing of my faith produces steadfastness...lacking in nothing! Wow. God is GOOD to me to give me this trial and I count it all joy! I want to stand this test to be blessed (James 1:12)

J—Wow. Love how God literally GIVES us verses specifically for our time of need. Makes me think of 2 Peter 1:3 "His divine power has granted to us all things that pertain to life and godliness, through the knowledge of him who called us to his own glory and excellence." You will one day look back and be amazed how God has grown you through this trial.

T—Whoa yes our partners verse!!! His power has been on complete display! I can already see the growth and shaping God is doing in me and my family the last 6 days. Feels like years of sanctification and trust. That's why I can count it all joy cause it's drawn me closer to the my living God. I can't wait to tell my mom everything God has done once she can handle it.

J—Awww it is such JOY. He is our Living Hope and JOY!!! Your mom will be amazed!! She has truly been a living sacrifice used for Gods GLORY!!!

T—Amen! I almost feel like the nurses and doctors are so confused at our joy and peace in this. It's incredible to know that when a major trial hits that I can cling to God and feel secure. I'm seriously in awe of the comfort and guidance of the Holy Spirit and all around me. He has not left me in my desperate time of need. I will never be alone. GLORY to Him and HIM ALONE! My precious Lord and my Holy God. And God has clearly spoken to me that I wasn't meant to have a child yet because of this. He wants me to be there for my dad and mom. So He answered that prayer clearly as to why I wasn't able to be a mommy yet. Cause I needed to be there for my mommy. I'm thankful that God revealed that to me.

J—Oh tiff i was literally thinking about this exact thing. If you were with child how could you have been there. Gods answers to our prayers are always perfect!! He knew you had something to do and He needed you for such a time as this!! So thankful so amazed at His love and mercy towards us. One of my favorite quotes by Helen Roseveare. (A missionary in Africa that had some horrific experiences there). The Question that came to her heart was, "Can you thank Me for trusting you with this experience even if I never tell you why?"[4]

T—Whoaaaa that's a really good quote. I feel blessed when God tells me why I'm going through something but He's God so he doesn't have to tell me! His ways are SO much higher than mine. I trust Him so deeply. I want to continue to trust and love Him more. I'm pumped up!

~*~

Jenni to Me..."Prayed you were so blessed by these conversations as we shared His miraculous Hand upon you, Vicki..."

"Indeed, we *[Apostle Paul and Timothy]* felt that we had received the sentence of death. But that was to make us rely not on ourselves but on God who raises the dead. He delivered us from such a deadly peril, and he will deliver us. On him we have set our hope that he will deliver us again. You also must help us by prayer, so that many will give thanks on our behalf for the blessings granted to us through the prayers of many." 2 Corinthians 1:9-11

~*~

July 14 @ 6:07 PM *(Saturday)*

She just responded to me when I asked and moved towards her. Blood pressure medication cut in half today with blood pressure dropping. She has tears when we are telling her we love her and God has done a miracle. She even did two blinks and a grimace when I asked her if I was the best husband. Please share. PTL...[Praise The Lord] Mike

July 16 @ 11:47 AM *(Monday)*

Compass prayer line... God continues to bless Vicki and her family and answer so many prayers. Vicki is now off the sedation meds. She is still going in and out of sleep a lot, but when she is awake, she is responding to yes and no questions with head nods. She is still on the ventilator, but they don't think she will need it for long! Prayer request... Vicki's major organs have required all the blood flow so her hands and feet have taken a hit. Please pray for Vicki's hands and feet to heal. Doctors and nurses have said that they could end up being amputated. Zoradi family believes that God can heal her hands and feet so that she can keep them. Please pray!

July 17 @ 9:58 AM *(Tuesday)*

Thank you so much to continue lifting her up in prayer. She's much more aware today and vitals improving and thus might go off the ventilator today... Thank you for not getting tired of endless continual prayer...Mike

July 18 @ 8:38AM *(Wednesday)*

Compass Prayer Line

Vicki is now off life support and her brain is doing well. She has excess fluids around her lungs right now. Doctors removed liquids from her lung today and they will do the other tomorrow. Please pray for this to solve the problem. Also, Vicki's hands and feet are still in very bad shape. Please continue to pray for God to allow regular blood flow to her extremities and for doctors not to have to amputate.

July 19 @ 6:38 PM *(Thursday)*

My prayer warriors...Vicki's heart, kidneys, and liver are all improving. She lacks strength in her abdomen to adequately cough up what she needs to from her lungs. Big prayers for that issue because the only other alternative is to put a trach in temporarily which is quite invasive. Please pass this on to everyone in HFG and thrive...Mike

July 21 @ 2:59 PM *(Saturday)*

Update...Vicki is very good today. Her blood pressure is stable. Her temperature is better. A little more awake. Pray she gets stronger. For Mike...continued good health, praying without ceasing, complete trust in God...

Woody and Darlene (HFG-Home Fellowship Group)

July 23rd @ 8:52 AM *(Monday)*

Good morning faithful prayer warriors! My heart is still full of praise to Our Heavenly Father for his faithfulness and immeasurable love for his children. I am overjoyed to hear about Vicki's progress and the fact that she could hear us last night... I pray for continued strength and peace for Vicki and you Mike. I am so encouraged by your faith and your praises to God, your love for your wife and your desire to give God all the glory. I am looking forward to welcoming Vicki back home and to hear her story!

Much love, Brigitte (HFG)

July 23 @ 7:51 PM

I agree with the understanding that only God could've pulled Vicki through. Blessings abound. Mike and Vicki you both have gone through this struggle, but we have been with you through prayer and heartache. Jesus had compassion on you both and undoubtedly greater things are due to happen. I pray it is first total healing of Vicki and His word will be revealed to others because of your steadfast love for Him.

41

Matthew 14:14 "When he [Jesus] went ashore, he saw a great crowd, and he had compassion on them and healed their sick."...

Love, Ron and Sue (HFG)

July 24 @ 10:32 AM *(Tuesday)*

Hey all... Thanks Ron and Sue for the prayers and encouragement. Vicki has continued to improve since our call on Sunday. She is having trach procedure done at 12 noon which will help the improvement and get her off the ventilator/tube. She is very excited to get rid of this tube. God bless you all. Sunday was very meaningful to Vicki and me...Mike

July 24 @ 11:04 AM

We will pray for the doctors to have a successful procedure and a quick recovery, and for Vicki to be able to breathe finally without the tube.

Irma and Nobu (HFG)

July 24 @ 3PM... Hey all my prayer warriors—Thanks much for lifting Vicki up in prayer. The procedure was successful with no complications — praise the Lord. She will be able to talk tomorrow and no tube which she will be excited about... Kidney Doctor said her kidney improvement has been great and might not need any more dialysis. Please pass on to Thrive people as well...Mike

July 25 @ 12:31 PM *(Wednesday)*

Vicki is doing well and looked the best ever today. Off life support and doing well with the trach. By tomorrow she could be talking but needs to do a swallow test to see if she can start eating soft foods. Pray for that step and her hands and feet. Thanks for all my prayer warriors!!!...Mike

July 25 @ 1:17 PM

We rejoice in the Lord for his goodness to allow Vicki to heal, to be able to begin taking soft food, and more important prayers for the blood to reach to her hands and feet to function normal. Love you Mike and Vicki, continue to pray for full recovery...

Nobuichi (HFG)

July 25 @ 2:22 PM

For the first time in three weeks, they are going to try to get her into a wheeling chair today. Her smile is full today and it made me cry. Pray that her body will accept heparin which reduces clots...and her hands and feet...Mike

July 25 @ 2:52 PM

Vicki, so grateful and joyful that you get to sit up and smile. You, Vicki, are such a blessing. I shared your story at the dentist office yesterday, pulled no punches that God had provided a miracle. Praise God. You have given me courage to be more bold.

Love you both, Sue (HFG)

July 25 @ 9:13 PM

Good evening prayer warriors... Just spoke to Mike tonight. It was the BEST day for Vicki. She was SUMMER VICKI with lots of smiles. Thank you LORD!!! She is still struggling with the liver. They decided to lower her dose and try another method of medication—please keep praying over this area. She was able to get in a chair and participate fully with one hour of PT. Praise. The nephrologist does not believe she will need any more dialysis, another praise. The next step is that Vicki will be transferred to an acute care rehab in Sacramento for a few days then transferred home to another acute rehab in Orange County . We have no timeline on this yet. Praying and waiting on the Lord for his plan and timing. A nurse commented to Mike today that Vicki is doing so well, we never see this. Mike said it's because Vicki has a lot of prayer backing her. She is a

43

Christian and totally agreed. So keep praying diligently over both of them. Mike has a lot of decisions ahead so pray for wisdom for him too.

Psalm 37:23 "The steps of a man are established by the LORD."

Psalm 116:1 "I love the LORD, because he has heard my voice and my pleas for mercy."

Keep those prayers coming...Mark and Jeanette (HFG Leaders)

July 26 @ 12:08 PM *(Thursday)*

I love the humor, Vicki has some humor herself. She has been winking at me. Praise the Lord! ...Mike

July 26 @ 8:32 PM

Compass prayer line... (URGENT) Vicki needs prayer for her last organ to recover (her liver). It's not doing well. She has a bilirubin of 27, but needs to get down around 20. This is a very serious need right now.

July 27 @ 11:44 AM *(Friday)*

Good morning prayer warriors,

Just spoke to Mike and wanted to share the latest so you can adjust your prayers. Vicki had another hour of PT yesterday. We're going to praise the Lord how well she is doing. The ability to turn her head and move her arms is huge. They are so very pleased with how well she is doing in this area. Her liver is struggling with clearing. Let's think about what has come at her in the last three weeks, a lot. But it's not too much for the Lord. The doctors believe there is more to the challenge than the clot in her liver. She has no fever, her blood pressure is good, heart is strong, kidneys strong, lungs are strong, Brain is great. She is conscious and mouthing words. WOW, that is amazing and we are to praise and give all glory to God. Mike thinks they may give her some dialysis to give her a little boost.

As we can all imagine that a season like this can test anyone's faith and it is a battle. Please lift up Mike! Doctors can be half-empty glass kind of guys at times. I've met many in my past. We know the Lord is so much bigger. Please pray for perseverance, strength, solid faith, energy, joy, and the mindset of honoring God through this trial. Please pray Mike will stay in the moment in faith. He read Luke 8:22-25. How Jesus calms the storm. Mike, Vicki, Mark and I we're on the Sea of Galilee. It's much bigger than I thought. Those seas could be fierce. But still he said, "Where is your faith?" Please keep praying to our most precious Heavenly Father who is absolutely holding all of this together. May HE continue to receive much GLORY. LORD, please open the eyes of these doctors and nurses. May they see and wonder. When there is wonder, there is always praise....

Love, Jeanette (HFG)

July 28 @ 5:52 PM *(Saturday)*

Here's another update from Mike today. Vicki has completed her fourth day of PT today. Today by Tiffani instead of the staff. Her bilirubin went down another point today. She is tolerating the medication necessary to deal with the liver clot. Same prayer requests, he's praising God for all the prayer warriors. Lots of praise to the LORD...

Mark and Jeanette (HFG)

July 29 @ 9:41 AM *(Sunday)*

Update... Several good things yesterday. Her bilirubin was down again – keep praying for that. She is tolerating the heparin which will work on her clot in her liver. She asked to go home which is the first time since day one. She said she will want to write a book to give God the glory. Please forward this everywhere...Mike

July 29 @ 3:11 PM

Vicki is doing well, her bilirubin went down again overnight 21. At 20 that would be a huge turn and ultimately it needs to be 12 before she can get out of ICU combined with eating food. Continue my prayer warriors. You are such a big part of this miracle and hopefully your prayer life and faith has increased like mine...Mike

July 30 @ 11:05 AM *(Monday)*

Vicki is doing great! Ever since the call for prayer for Bilirubin, it has gone down from 27 to 19. Our God is the Great Physician! Having a procedure at 3pm to put a feeding tube into stomach that will allow for transfer from ICU. Spoke her first words today… Guess??? Praise God...Mike

July 30 @ 5:39 PM

That was beautiful and lifted my spirits… Vicki moved her fingers on her left hand for the first time today. Praise God!!! Mike

~*~

AUGUST

August 1 @ 1:25 PM *(Wednesday)*

Heading to see Mike and Vicki in a bit. Mike said they put a flap in the trach and she talked for about 15 minutes. They took it back out after 15. Excited!

Mark (HFG Leader)

August 1 @ 9:59 PM

Hello family. We wanted to share with you our first day with Mike and Vicki. She looks like beautiful Summer Vicki! She was sitting in a special chair-like bed. She is using her trach very well. Able to cough out fluids. A little jaundice but getting better with each day with her Bilirubin numbers declining. They removed her catheter today, another praise. They received word today that Sutter Memorial is working on transferring her to Hoag Hospital acute rehab in Newport. They're thinking it could be this very

Friday. Such a praise. They both are ready to go home. Mike will follow the ambulance to Hoag. Insurance will cover this, another praise.

Today they told Mike, one day in ICU equals one week of rehab. So we have quite a recovery. Met amazing nurses, they all love her. She is sleeping a lot. Please please pray fervently for her hands and feet. She showed me today how she can move some of her fingers on her left hand. She's winking and smiling. Glad she's not having any more procedures. She has been through a great deal. Seeing her today put things in perspective. Fragile and vulnerable. A beautiful visit with her. Met her sister and brother-in-law today. They live 30 minutes from the hospital. They come daily! This is where Mike has been sleeping. Mike is resting in God's strength. He was showing us how he wets her lips and teeth with a sponge very often. He's able to give her ice chips. She is so excited about ice chips. He is caring for her very well. Please keep praying over all these details. It appears we will all be able to visit her soon and often...

Jeanette and Mark

August 2 @ 2:44 PM *(Thursday)*

Prayer. As Vicki is becoming more awake, she's also experiencing pain. She had speech and physical therapy today. They gave her mild sedation to help with her pain. Thank you...

Jeanette

August 3 @ 2:32 PM *(Friday)*

It is concentrated prayer time again. Vicki's white blood cell count is up again. It appears she has another bladder infection. Please be praying. They will not be transferring her today. Taking a step back and making sure she is stable for the long ride. Thank you for your prayers...

Jeanette

August 9 @ 9:14 AM *(Thursday)*

I have another update from Mike as of this morning. Praise they have been accepted to Kindred Hospital Westminster. This is a 109 bed transitional care hospital offering the same in-depth care you would receive in a traditional hospital, but for an extended recovery period. Praise their insurance company just approved this morning. Now please be praying for the ambulance, transfer, hands and feet, and the second season of this walk of faith. Praise that Vicki ate real food yesterday with the trach still in place. With the flap, Vicki is talking all day long. Lord, we are giving You all the glory, honor and praise. We have seen you work in so many powerful ways during the season.

Psalm 71:14 "But I will hope continually and will praise you yet more and more."

Psalm 106:8 "Yet he saved them for his name's sake, that he might make known his mighty power."

Mark and Jeanette

August 9 @ 9:47 PM

Mike and Vicki, we are so thankful for your return tomorrow to the OC! We are praying for your travels and all of the transition to go smoothly, and for God to use the staff at this new facility to provide excellent care for your recuperation! When you are ready, we look forward to seeing you soon!

Love, Woody and Darlene (HFG)

August 10 @ 11:31 PM *(Friday)*

We wanted each of you to know that Vicki arrived to the acute rehabilitation center at Westminster today late afternoon. Mike was very pleased with the facility. Said it was very clean and the staff was very friendly. Once they got Vicki settled, the main Doctor who will be caring for her called Mike. He's from Irvine Medical Center in Orange. He plans to see her tomorrow and assess her needs. He mentioned to Mike that he and his team are very aggressive and have many ideas to treat her hands and feet. Mike said he was hopeful. Please pray for this visit tomorrow and wisdom regarding her feet and hands. Thank you for praying...

Mark and Jeanette

~*~

One month of these coveted prayers and communications were unknown to me until my friend Jeanette presented me with a huge binder full of these emails and more. Tears of joy flowed as I read every word.

This first leg of my tragic journey so far had come to a close. I titled this part of my life's obstacle course *HWY 50's FRIGHTENING FREEWAY*. The starting line's Green Flag for me waved. The race to wellness began on a most memorable day at our lovely, pine-wood family cabin in the mountains. I then revved my engine, punched the gas pedal, took off, and rushed onward to Marshall Hospital in Placerville. It was a very short pit stop in the historic gold mining town. But, in Sacramento (Sacra-Tomato), my car finally stalled out completely at Sutter Memorial's ICU Trauma Center.

I soon realized that those paralyzing pitfalls and health emergencies endured in Northern California would be extended far into this upcoming lap. *CALIFORNIA's PRECARIOUS INTERSTATE 5 EXPRESSWAY* was labeled by me (and possibly many other race drivers who experienced my level of symptoms of infection and toxicity).

To be honest, I was fearful of the unknown that laid entirely out of my reach back home, especially with hands that no longer functioned. I had not yet begun this part of my Southern California overhaul. But when I needed additional help in Orange County, my Heavenly Driver pulled me quickly off the expressway. He down-shifted into lower second gear, steered toward the closest open service station, and cut my engine before a fire could ignite.

Time for a necessary service stop. I handed over my 'keys' once again to the top-rated Mechanic possible—*The Great Physician*—my Lord Jesus Christ.

Complete overhaul—which included unbelievable struggles and downtime— awaited me in Southern California. My *'ride'* required multiple repairs. On the service contract: A tune-up, new tires, different timing belt, well-deserved lube and oil change, also significant bodywork were necessary.

But, before I signed any contract, it was required to discover how God—in his infinite wisdom and sovereignty—had prepared us for this fire-burning trial decades ago. Come along with me as we travel back in time... *'Back To The Future'*... [5]

BUT GOD...

"Then the magicians said to Pharaoh, 'This is the finger of God.'" Exodus 8:19

"But truly God has listened; he has attended to the voice of my prayer." Psalm 66:19

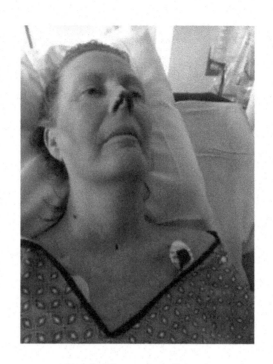

Can't Move Anything!

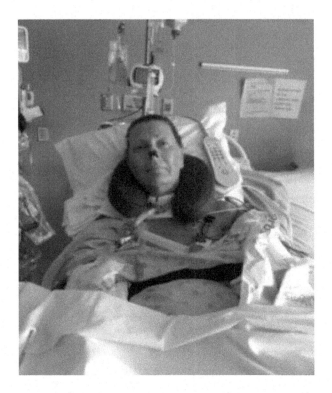

Semi-Conscious at Sutter Memorial in Sacramento

Awakened To Mike's Comfort—My Rock, My Love

CHAPTER 3

PROVIDENTIAL PLANS & PURPOSES

"...that they may see and know, may consider and understand together, that the hand of the LORD has done this, the Holy One of Israel has created it." Isaiah 41:20

"For we are his workmanship, created in Christ Jesus for good works, which God prepared beforehand, that we should walk in them." Ephesians 2:10

We never saw what God had prepared us for until we looked back in the rearview mirror over the last four decades. We visualized how God's mighty hand had providentially worked out each detail of our lives for His purposes. After we found ourselves in this major health crisis, neither Mike nor I could have ever fathomed how our lives changed directly and permanently. There were several key factors that God supremely used to *"tune up"* our lives. As we looked back, He faithfully prepared us for this fiery trial.

It reminded me of Exodus 3:12 when God told Moses, in part, *"I will be with you!"* God had prepared Moses for 40 years in the nomadic land of Midian as a shepherd of sheep and goats. He tackled the most challenging job ever asked of him. He went before Pharaoh and demanded that he "Let God's people go."

Well, Mike and I have been married for 40 years! We looked back over these last four decades and received a glimpse of just how The Preeminent God arranged and predestined our journey of faith.

God—The All-Knowledgeable—had been in control from our inception.

Our intertwined lives felt much like we lived in America's first parlor game—"*The Game of Life*"®—originally created in 1860 by Milton Bradley. The modern version that we knew and loved as kids was revised 100 years later by Rueben Klamer and Bill Markham [1]. Each player began by choosing a little plastic, colored car with either a candy-pink human peg (female) or sky-blue peg (male). Once selected, it was placed in the car's driver's seat then situated on the starting line. Sometimes referred to only as "*Life*," this board game mimicked our adventurous travels through our forty-five years of togetherness. Many years have passed since I have played 'LIFE' with childhood friends. In the current version, players even adopt pets that ride along with them on their courageous trip towards the board's finish line.

As a young player, I had placed my bright pink car token and light pink driver's peg at the starting line. I then spun the onboard spinner (1-10) and embarked on an imaginary journey through life. I traveled along through small mountains, around buildings and passed other landmarks, features, and entertainment adventures. My randomly chosen 'life' unfolded as I proceeded to advance my car around the racetrack. Throughout the game, each of my friends also made critical decisions for their own lives. We all hoped to emerge the champion driver of the "*Game of Life®.*"

Our decisions were mixed with random spins and action card selections. These 99 Action Cards made for a fun-filled journey of laughter and amusement. Each hoped that their choices led them on a quick, smooth pace towards the checkered flag!

But, some spins or cards drove our cars through pitfalls, bumpy roads full of dangers, or hazardous perils that each of us encountered along our way. The game's object was to get one's car on the fastest, easiest path of least resistance and reach the journey's end in record time. As I sped towards the finish line, I often **was** the most successful driver. I had collected the highest bank account at the finish line and, therefore, won the game.

I wish to share our early *Life* experiences together and reveal precisely how God directed our journey through these forty-plus years. It has been quite an adventurous life with Mike Zoradi. Such love. Such commitment. I used various MILESTONES—though not in chronological order—to reveal our lives' beginnings and God's providential plan. I hope that this blast from the past is a most enjoyable ride.

Pre-Mike Zoradi—1974

HIGH SCHOOL/DATING:

I'm convinced God created and chose Mike just for me. God providentially planned for Mike to marry me and become my spouse. When I met Mike Zoradi, I was still Vicki Rene' Patterson. On a Tuesday, August 19th of 1975, we met at a summer church camp called Silver Spur Christian Camp & Retreat Center in Tuolumne, California. I first laid my baby blues on him after early roll call and breakfast that morning. He was playing a pick-up game of touch football with a bunch of guys.

He was fast. He was athletic. And he was cute. But, he was too far away to catch his eye. Mike seemed very comfortable as he played the positions of wide receiver and sometimes quarterback. He caught most everything thrown his way by my friend, Drew, the quarterback. They had called this guy 'Zoradi' [zor-Ah'-dee] who just so happened to be on the winning team.

After the football game, Mike bee-lined straight for me. He introduced himself. *Bold!* I liked it. We both chatted a minute with Drew before my friend winked at me and left us alone. Mike sat down fairly close to me under a large pine tree while we got to know each other a slight bit better.

Mike shared a short version of his testimony when he handed over his life to Jesus Christ at age sixteen the summer before. His faith was obviously on fire for God! He explained how he surrendered his life and will to Jesus Christ. This monumental decision to follow Jesus occurred at Young Life's Woodleaf Christian High School Camp in the foothills of Northern California. He no longer lived for himself. He had repented and placed his total trust in Jesus's finished work on the cross.

After Mike finished, I shared my salvation story, too. I had become a Christian earlier in my life—fifth grade. As our conversation continued, my girlfriends from church and my sister, Valori, asked me to come to hang out with them in the chapel. We said our fast good-byes with dazzling smiles. *(Mike's dad was an orthodontist).* I left to join them while Mike trekked off to his cabin to take a shower and get cleaned up.

Our next face-to-face was an hour or so later when Zoradi walked into chapel...

My senses were heightened. Mike pulled up a chair by my side of the couch and introduced himself all the way around. He was not one bit shy. Extremely confident. But yet again, within ten minutes, I was needed elsewhere. I arose off the couch and walked out alone. *Oh no*, I thought, *I just exited and left this handsome boy with all of my attractive church friends. What was I thinking!?*

This day was packed with terrific memories. Two more happened later that same day. I had left the chapel to go to the sizable 300-seat auditorium where the entire camp's crowd met each morning and evening for devotions and sermon talks. I played the piano and accompanied our church's small youth choir for a special Worship Night. It was roughly between 3-4 pm. We held practice with two of the lead singers and backup vocalists after lunch.

But once we got the Gospel music down for that evening, Drew began rockin' out with drum sticks on his Levi®□ jeans. He sang emphatically into his mic, lyrics to some 70's tunes that I played from memory— Chicago's *'Saturday in the Park'* [2] and *'Let It Be'* [3] by The Beatles. While Drew loudly crooned away and others gathered up their stuff to leave, I glanced up when the door flew open. My heartbeat raced out of my chest when I saw my future husband—at seventeen—as he walked towards me. He boldly sat down smack-dab up next to me on the piano bench. He proceeded to ask me, "Do you mind if I stay and turn your pages for you?" It was funny because Mike knew absolutely nothing about music, let alone sheet music. But there he was. And I was thrilled!

Mike is one hilarious person. He proved it to me later that same day. After dinner and followed by the fantastic evening sermon from Josh McDowell, all campers began to pair off into smaller groups of twos, threes, or fours. The church's youth leaders had scheduled campers to play the game *Hunt for Counselors* in the dark on the wooded hills. Flashlights were optional. While we finished our desserts of Popsicles and brownies, many kids had congregated around.

Since Mike was reasonably new to the church, he only knew a handful of campers that attended his high school. There was a relatively large mixed group of about ten to twelve students who stood in the outside spotlight, which beamed down off the kitchen's roof. Two of his classmates knew Mike, so he felt comfortable as we discussed arrangements of the guy/girl groups. The leaders did not want girls to go out alone in the dark woods. So, at least one male had to be in each group, unless a group had a minimum of six girls that stayed together. Safety came first, of course.

One of the boys point-blank asked me—in front of everyone present—"Hey Vicki, do you want to go with me to find counselors in the dark?" I must have hesitated for a split second before I answered because Mike immediately moved over to me and confidently announced, "Sorry, Dude, she's going with me."

Shocked!

We locked eyes in the spotlight before I quickly responded, "Yep, sorry, I'm going with Mike." We grabbed hands and left the rest in our dust as we ran to get a head start on the game.

A year earlier, at sixteen years old, I prayed in earnest for God to send my way a Christian, God-fearing, Bible-believing guy to court for marriage. I wrote down 26 non-negotiable character traits mixed with some of my own heart desired attributes. I met Mike Zoradi one year later. Even way back then, God had chosen to bless me with Mike. He became a predestined mate for me.

We had gone to rival high schools, but God made sure we attended the same Baptist Church in Sacramento, California. God also pre-ordained that we both were campers together who desired to know one another that summer week. Mike had broken up with his non-Christian girlfriend at the end of his junior year of high school. And I had not found anyone that fit my list of dating qualifications. Was this to be a camp romance that fizzled out after we returned home?

[I came across the tattered binder-paper list several years after marriage. Mike fulfilled all 26 of my dating conditions and heart desires.]

59

Moments after I had walked into my house from camp, I was providentially informed by an acceptance letter that my senior-year Regional Occupational Program (ROP) would *"just so happen"* to be held at Mike's high school. *Would this fact make us or break us?* I questioned. I knew if it broke us up, then God had someone better in mind for me.

I revealed—tenuously—this ROP location and its time schedule with Mike after picking me up for the Sunday evening church service. This new boyfriend, with great excitement, twirled me around. He was so thrilled. Destiny. Mike had a plan all figured out within minutes. Three times a week, Mike drove to my school in his classic 1966 Mustang. After we stopped to eat lunch, he drove us to his school's front parking lot. Mike went straight to basketball practice while I attended ROP insurance classes at the same time. We met back together on the Senior Lawn before he drove me home. Perfect Plan.

Before we met each other's families, we had finished that warm Indian summer dating and carefree. Mike painted houses. I worked at Gunther's Ice Cream shop [4]. Other than that, we spent eight- to ten-hour days inseparable. We began our senior year of high school within two weeks.

I learned pretty quickly that Mike's mom suffered terribly from chronic migraine headaches. Since Mike was the last and only child who still lived at home, he unwaveringly helped his dad care for his mom when needed. Mike had such a tender heart and stepped in to help with whatever his mom desired. He accomplished everything his dad required of him. It was not an easy task for a seventeen-year-old male to give personal attention to a loved one. Just as God had called Moses through a burning bush in Exodus 3, Mike was unaware that God called and prepared him for his significant caregiver role for me 45 years later.

Mike and I had a fantastic first year of dating throughout our senior year of high school. We enjoyed football and basketball games, dances, pizza, our favorite Jimboy's Tacos [5], concerts, holidays, and Senior Ball at his school. We celebrated our *"togetherness"* on the 19th of every month that first year. Most gifts exchanged between us had been spiritual in nature. We both realized that this relationship was unique. We put God at the center. Love had grown stronger with each fleeting season. Mike and I appreciated that God allowed us this year of joyous harmony before college separation. As our exuberant youth and lighthearted times slowly wound down, we graduated high school in June of 1976.

COLLEGE:

High school graduation had passed, and summer was at its peak. What lodged in the back of our minds was the fact that Mike would head off to college way too soon. Westmont College is located in Southern California's beach town of Santa Barbara in Montecito Hills. Both his brothers had graduated from and met their wives at this small, donated estate, Christian college.

Our families at the time were glad that we had let our dating options remain open once we parted. They believed we were too young at seventeen to be so attached emotionally with such a distance between us. So, we did *not* commit to date exclusively throughout our first year of college. Our relationship was then defined. Open Border. We were free to date others.

My brother, Mike 'Pats', did not end up with his high school sweetheart after attending Trinity Western College in Canada. He met and later married his love, Brenda. Zoradi brothers married Westmont girls—not their high school flings. Mike and I both figured that, even though we could date others, that conscious decision opened us up to God's Will of whom HE wanted us to marry.

So, I felt God had constructed just for me a vast, impassable roadblock. It wouldn't have been clearer if it had a flashing neon signposted, which blinked—DO NOT ENTER! It pointed definitively to Mike's departure during this higher educational turnpike.

Mike took off late August and got settled in as our summer break of love diminished. He drove that day towards Santa Barbara in his sister Yvonne's hand-me-down 1967 restored dark green Volkswagen Bug. My boyfriend—now an absent love—drove the lonely 393-mile trip without me. I already felt so empty without him. My heart was excited about Mike's new adventure but deeply saddened for me. This separation was a clean break. We pledged to call once a week and write our love notes and letters. Yet, we both prayed that another love would not replace us.

After I wiped away a few tears, I began my long local junior college path. Mike came to visit once a month around his school breaks. His first visit produced extra excitement when I walked out of my trigonometry class in late October. Mike Zoradi was as handsome as ever! He had waited just for me, and we were still in love. Although, deep inside, I still guarded my heart against breakage. The thought loomed deeply in my soul that Mike may still find someone else.

Would he forget all about me? Could he?

We talked once a week by telephone—pre-cell phones—as promised. Mike phoned from a 1977-aged telephone booth located just outside Westmont's tiny Post Office. I was upstairs in my parents' condominium tucked away in the master bathroom so my younger sister couldn't eavesdrop. Half an hour from 11:00-11:30 pm cost a reduced rate of $10. We would split the cost since we both worked part-time. Every week, the chats were planned much like a scheduled dinner date. Unless, of course, he came home for a quick visit.

Mike asked me to join him at Westmont College for the upcoming sophomore year's fall semester. Without God's intervention, there was no way. Money was the central issue. One year at Westmont costs as much as purchasing an automobile. The most exciting news arrived in the mail at the end of our Freshmen year. I had applied for a full scholarship and received 100% funding for my tuition.

Praise God.

Although, I also needed a job on campus and a low-interest loan that paid for room and board. I worked that year as an assistant to President Dr. Winter's secretary *'Mrs. Efficient'* in the Kerr Hall Administration Building. Typing was my specialty. Both of us indeed enjoyed that sophomore year—hand in hand—as we knocked down our second collegiate year. But, unfortunately, that togetherness at Westmont did not extend into our days as juniors.

Without the scholarship funds, I returned home to Sacramento because I needed a job. Mike came home as well. He realized that Sacramento State University had an outstanding Business Department. Why had he spent a higher dollar amount of his parents' money to go to a private school when he didn't need to? Great justification.

We both remained at our own family homes to save money before marriage. Our carefree lifestyles had vanished. On the horizon, full-time work to support me and save while Mike was a full-time student and part-time employee. God paved our way. We felt God's blessing, so we continued onto the path of least resistance—a spring wedding.

MARRIAGE:

"Therefore, a man shall leave his father and mother and hold fast to his wife, and the two shall become one flesh." Ephesians 5:31

Mike proposed marriage to me a week before Christmas Day in 1978. Firehouse Restaurant's candlelit meal in old town Sacramento by the train museum, bouquet of roses, romantic fire at his place, and dessert was arranged. Alone. No huge fanfare or photos as couples out-perform one another in anticipation of 'the big question' nowadays. Mike knew my reply would be "yes" even before he posed the question. He was on his 6-week holiday break from his junior year at Sac State. We married in the former

Arcade Baptist Church in Sacramento's 103° heat on May 26, 1979, @ 3 pm.

Married to Mike Zoradi at age 20, I gave God all credit for my customized personality. Over time, I had transformed into an extrovert like him. Mike always talked to strangers as if he had known them his entire life. Once, he spoke to someone at the airport as if they had been childhood friends. The two talked, joked around, slapped hands on the back, etc. When they parted with waves and smiles, I questioned Mike, "Who was that?" He quipped back nonchalantly, "Oh, I don't know? Why?" I just shook my head with amazement once again.

Mike was not even aware that he put others at ease with his low-key, light-hearted, loudly fun conversations. That was what shaped him to be such a fabulous salesman, co-worker, friend, sports' enthusiast, mentor, evangelist. But more than any of those, Mike's a tremendous life-partner, son-in-law, brother, husband, father, and grandfather.

A new experimental medication came on our radar just after marriage. I suffered from a painful endometriosis diagnosis pre-wedding at age 18. My ob/GYN, who delivered me and played golf with Mike's dad, was hesitant. Not that he didn't want to prescribe it, but he knew the price tag was steep, especially for newlyweds. He asked us gingerly, "How much do you pay monthly for your condo's mortgage?" *(He was so fatherly towards us.)* After we responded with the dollar amount, he explained further, "Now quadruple it! That's how astronomically priced your medication will cost you each month. For that reason, I didn't mention it."

*[—Just for comparison as if it happened today...A South Orange County 2-bedroom condo rental —for the duplicate square footage away from the coast—costs today approximately $2,450 per month. My prescription for the present day's price tag would be $2,450 (quadrupled) = $9,800 PER MONTH! That's roughly $82 per pill, $328 per day every day. For the eighteen-month regimen's **grand total**, we would have been looking at $176,400+ if it were currently happening now.]*

64

The doctor was correct. WE couldn't afford it, but Retail Clerks' Teamsters Union insurance program could, and they did. Mike worked part-time at a local grocery store and brought home money while he attended school full-time. Our bill for the medication mentioned above after my examination was only $5/month! Four pills a day cleared up my female insides; nine months on/nine months off/nine months on again. I loved this medication. Not only did it take away my monthly pain problem, but it also caused more muscle mass (*shapely calf muscles*), I sang tenor with the men in our church choir, and I felt stronger, more resilient. The negative: it caused motion sickness when we traveled. It was well worth the $45 for nine months. $90 **Grand Total**. God showed up in our crosswalk. He had been so kind, gracious, and faithful. He cared for His children as our Crossing Guard, who ushered us safely across this busy intersection.

CAREERS:

ROP had trained me well in the field of insurance. While I assisted my newlywed husband financially in his career path, he completed his final undergraduate year at Cal State Sacramento. Mike also attained his MBA from Golden Gate University. I worked full-time from 1978 to the end of 1984. I climbed the Worker's Compensation ladder from file clerk to underwriter.

Mike's career road, after he obtained his Masters of Business Administration, qualified him for many open doors. Pre-kids, he worked for Lanier Corporation. He sold business office machines. Their training program was excellent as they honed Mike's sales skills. But this problematic job description constantly required him to '*cold call*' for new clients. Even though successful, Mike desired to work with a team. So, he joined a sales team for Glasrock Home Healthcare with the Sacramento, Yuba City, Chico, Redding territories. God guided, and Mike was equipped for this next step. We stayed put in Sacramento next to all my family members and Mike's parents. Our best-laid plans cruised us along uneventfully.

We had put in an offer on an established home close to Sacramento's American River Drive. Their realtor rejected our offer. *What?* We questioned, *Why?* Another couple also had put in their offer that Saturday. Only a measly half hour before us. We were late by 30 minutes. *Are they sure?* We were stunned. We just missed our chance.

Why God? Is it not Your plan? We trust You in all things.

We found out the answer to our why question one month later. God pulled our spark plugs! He placed our car on a different track. Mike was offered a sales management position that had recently materialized in Southern California territory—from San Diego to Thousand Oaks. He grabbed at the promotion. We hadn't anticipated this move to the southern part of the state. But, Omniscient God knew in advance. *Thank you, Heavenly Father, that our offer had **not** gone through.* I would have been stuck up north trying to sell our 'new' home while Mike was south looking for a rental.

Mike, however, was soon stolen away to work for Medcom, Inc.[6] in 1989 when the owner made his former boss CEO. My wonderful husband was promoted once again to Vice President of Sales and Marketing. Eventually, in 2016, he became their CEO. This healthcare company trains and provides Continuing Education credits to U.S. hospital personnel—physicians, surgeons, specialists, PAs, BSNs and RNs, LVNs, and CNAs.

Even though he never went through medical school, Mike's medical background proved very valuable while we drove through my physically perilous hospitals' land mines. My body was damaged. My life dangled by a thin thread. But, our Immeasurable God was still in charge.

FAMILY:

"Like arrows in the hand of a warrior are the children of one's youth. Blessed is the man who fills his quiver with them!..." Psalm 128:4-5a

In our life, we chose to grow our marital union and practiced having children after Mike completed his MBA. He was already launched well into his career. When we made that monumental decision, we were both 24-years-old at that time. Our desire was to no longer work outside the home for me once kids began to cover our landscape. We had been married for four years.

I got pregnant after endometrial treatment at age 24, which then was a piece of cake. But, keeping the babies in utero proved much more difficult. I had my first of three miscarriages at ten weeks gestation. But we were delighted that God chose to bless us at twenty-six with a son on Christmas Eve of 1984. *David Tyler Zoradi.* David is a solid biblical name. David was also my brother's and Mike's brother's middle names. He was known as *'Davy Jones'* as a youngster by family and *'Dave'* now that he's an adult. We placed a sky-blue peg in our plastic car and kept our car on Parents Path for several years. I had left the insurance industry after David arrived. I was a fortunate stay-at-home mom until the mid-1990s. If I picked three adjectives to describe David, they would be kind-hearted, loyal, and attentive. He is a loving son, grandson, brother, husband to his wife Keana, and father to Jet William and newborn Eden Joy.

We spun the spinner again two years later, but two more early miscarriages led to frequent prayers, confusion, and heartache. It wasn't until Mike's company—*rather God*—transferred us to Mission Viejo in Southern California when David was 2-1/2 years old. My OB doctor *'Dr. Un Cer-Tain'* in Sacramento during that season of life just kept shrugging his shoulders while he passed on to us his medical knowledge that 25% of all pregnancies end in miscarriage. He was obviously not a high-risk pregnancy specialist.

God had other plans. He showed me a new doctor who had a thriving infertility practice at Mission Hospital in Mission Viejo named *'Doctor Optimistically Kool.'* Just in a matter of moments after I shared my OB history with him, he knowingly spoke, "Luckily, you are not having difficulty getting pregnant, as do most of my patients. Next time you believe you are pregnant, come in straight away for pregnancy and progesterone tests. I suspect that you are losing these babies because you are low in the progesterone needed to carry your babies to term."

Was it that easy?

It appeared so. Within the next two months, I found I was again pregnant and likewise petrified. *Would I lose this baby as well?* I quickly scheduled the blood tests. For results, back in 1988, I went downstairs to the records department at Mission Hospital's basement level, showed my identification, and a medical technician read my results right there on the spot.

Yes, I was pregnant again. *Joy!* But, my jubilance was short lived. The progesterone count was at four. The caring technician explained to me that this was NOT good news. I began to shake nervously and asked him, "What does a 'four' mean?" He told me calmly, "Four is a low, low count. For a pregnancy to be viable, that four should be at a minimum of 20. Call your doctor before you head home."

Suffice it to say, I immediately called *'Dr. O.K.'* He advised me not to go home yet, but to drive to my nearest pharmacy and pick up a prescription for pure progesterone that he would call in promptly. It was ready within minutes after arrival. I gladly administered these daily for the next three weeks. At nine weeks in the womb, the baby had already begun to produce what she needed for survival. God held our pregnancy situation in his mighty hands, again for His glory and our joy.

On November 2nd, 1988, we welcomed our final baby, who was barely born on her due date right before midnight. *Tiffani Rene' Zoradi.* Tiffani means *"Light of God."* Rene' is French which stands for someone who is *"Reborn"* or *"Born Again."* Rene' is my middle name, and I've always liked it—Tiff not so much. Now our car felt full after we added a candy-pink peg in the backseat. Tiffani is a caring daughter, granddaughter, sister, wife, mother to Cal, and friend. My choice of three adjectives that describe Tiff would be compassionate, friendly, generous. Mike and I currently hold fast to the future hope that we will meet and hug our other three children in heaven someday.

COLLEGE & CAREER UPDATE:

"Whatever you do, work heartily, as for the Lord and not for men, knowing that from the Lord you will receive the inheritance as your reward. You are serving the Lord Christ." Colossians 3:24

Before the foundations of the earth, God planned that I would one day become a grade-school teacher for over 20 years. God gave me His stamp of approval to abandon my pre-kids insurance career. He changed my educational course at a pivotal crossroad toward a licensed California teacher. As I began to pray about this change, the Lord sent a confirmation to me in several ways.

The first confirmation came when David entered kindergarten. I began to volunteer each Friday afternoon to assist his teacher while a church friend watched one-year-old Tiffani. Her son was David's church buddy, and we would swap hours in our free church's Christian Babysitting Co-op. His kindergarten teacher put me in various teaching small group roles. I quickly began to pull aside small groups for reading, writing, or mathematics instruction while she kept busy as she instructed or monitored her other students.

I wondered why I had been given such a highly valued volunteer position. I found out why that next week. "You're a teacher, aren't you?" When I told her that I wasn't, she expressed, "Well, you should be!" After 900 volunteer hours and fulfilled roles of PTO Treasurer and Co-President, I followed God's track. He had chosen for me to become a California Licensed K-8 Multiple Subject Teacher. So, I had pressed onward towards that goal.

Another confirmation came while God prepared me for the teaching arena. It had to do with all my class time slots and schedules. When David was in school all day, and Tiff was three, I returned to a local college two mornings a week to complete my undergraduate work in Liberal Studies. I enrolled in Mission Viejo's Saddleback College. I didn't want our family's lives to be adversely impacted due to scheduling conflicts. All-Sovereign Lord worked my college class schedule precisely in conjunction with our kids' pre-school and grade school schedules.

Mike's job required a 45-minute daily, high-traffic commute and a few overnight travels once or twice a month for over 30 years. I needed to be the parent responsible and available to pick the kids up if necessary. *Hmmm.* No shock that all my class schedules those years perfectly gelled with their school schedules.

Saddleback's campus included a portion leased out to Cal State Fullerton. This location made my transfer to university a much smoother endeavor. It also allowed me to stay close to home right up to my final graduation year. My senior year's seven classes at CSUF's campus *(25.8 miles one-way)* coincided with Tiffani's kindergarten debut. I registered for three in the fall and the final four in the spring. But once again, I needed a sitter for 1-2 hours after our neighborhood school was dismissed in the afternoon. A new fabulous kindergarten mother/friend I met that year stepped up to help. Pamela looked for supplemental income while I desperately searched for a loving sitter. Perfect fit. That year went off without one interruption or glitch.

Tiffani's childcare at age five was now covered. David, four years older, walked with his friend to his house after school. They played or started their homework until I got home an hour later. I loved being my children's mom in those early impressionable days; it brought me extreme joy. I cruised into the final lap of teaching preparation.

"The heart of man plans his way, but the LORD establishes his steps."
Proverbs 16:9

Green flag down. White flag in sight...

1991—Young Thirties

PROFESSION:

But before I could move an inch forward, I *NEEDED* God to clear an enormously huge obstacle on my course before I could enter the final lap. I needed to acquire a guaranteed spot in the coveted CSUF Student Teacher's Credential Program. Requirements to be considered were: Graduate degree in Childhood Development or Liberal Studies—ON YOUR MARK. Minimum GPA 3.6—GET SET. One hundred minimum volunteer hours with grade school-aged children—GO! I hand-delivered my application, prayed for God's Will to be revealed, then moved strategically to the front of the pack as I continued this race to finish strong. At age 38, by the grace of God, I was chosen. I knew then that The Almighty had cleared the track.

God confirmed once again his career choice for me—Public School Teacher. With my final lap ahead of me, I would not receive the winner's trophy until this required, extensive year of Student Teaching was in my rearview mirror as well. The year consisted of two student-teacher assignments in the community, plus I had to pass the Multiple Subject Assessment for Teachers—*MSAT*. God thankfully provided his guidance.

My first semester of student teaching was in 2nd grade with two Master Teachers. The second semester—6th grade. By happenstance, Tiffani was in 2nd grade, and David was in 6th. I passed. *Woo-Hoo!* Checkered flag wildly waved May 1996 as I crossed this teacher's finish line.

I always cherished my career as a part-time/full-time, multi-subject elementary school teacher. I strove to shape all of my former students. My goal for each was: To become highly educated, well-rounded, good citizens who became lovers of reading and mathematics. Some are now married with children of their own. When God called me into teaching, He equipped me.

During these two professions—Worker's Compensation Underwriter and Elementary School Teacher—I conducted business with agents, CEOs,

72

managers, underwriters and students, parents, principals, and staff. Thus it allowed me many opportunities to speak to various small and large groups of people without that fear that most people get when public speaking. God changed my persona. I used to be a reasonably shy teen who blossomed into an extrovert by the time I approached my thirties.

I so relished my speaking engagements. I appreciated one-on-one with students, whole-class instruction, colleague meetings, and lead musical performances with 150 students. Also, I thoroughly enjoyed meeting my students' parents. I discussed their child's yearly goals and accomplishments. I conducted many Back to School Nights, parent conference weeks, student-generated musicals, and Open House evenings. The more listeners I had, the more I enjoyed speaking.

SPECIALIZED TRAINING:

"All scripture is breathed out by God and profitable for teaching, for reproof, for correction, and for training in righteousness, that the man of God may be complete, equipped for every good work." 2 Timothy 3:16-17

Punch the gas pedal a few decades and fast forward to 2009. Another detail that God proved that He was the One steering our car was regarding our daughter Tiffani. After her two-year college courses—organic chemistry, macro-and micro-biology, and physiology—Tiffani began her nursing program. These classes were all required when choosing a career in healthcare. After shadowing a nurse in her program, Tiff came to me one day and shared that she had not felt that becoming a nurse was a good fit for her. She had not had a chance to work one-to-one with patients as much as she had desired. My first thought was, *Oh no, all those classes and time down the drain.* But, as an experienced mom at that time, I held my tongue.

Concurrently, I had a special needs child in my fourth-grade class, and my district had paid for me to attend a related conference. One of the instructors had her Master of Science degree in Speech Therapy. I went up to her at the break and asked, "If you had the chance all over again, would you still choose to become a speech therapist, or would you have chosen a different career path?"

She chuckled, "*Hands-down,* I would have become an occupational therapist." When I asked her why? She replied, "Because I would work one-on-one with patients, get paid a fantastic salary, and also OTs can write their own ticket because there are not very many of them. I could work in a hospital setting, a school setting, a rehab facility, pediatrics, or a skilled nursing facility. The possibilities are endless."

I thanked her for her honesty and immediately went outside. I texted Tiffani and told her to check out *'Occupational Therapy'* and what that career path would entail. She was excited to look it up. She shared with me later that this was a perfect career path for her, precisely the one she desired. Her studies would not be wasted.

Little did I know then that Tiffani would graduate with her undergraduate degree and her 2-year Masters in Occupational Therapy six months before I needed her desperately to work with me as I learned to use my new prosthetic limbs.

What professional did I need most besides a prosthetist?...

An Occupational Therapist!

Master of OT Graduation—January 2018

Tiffani was licensed with the State of California two months before my gruesome plight began. God is so good, isn't he? I praise him for his faithfulness to arrange Tiff's essential educational plan *FOUR YEARS* before her vital expertise was needed to work with me.

Also, in God's unique plan, Tiffani had been trying to have a baby a few years after she married Mike Washburn. They couldn't understand why she wasn't able to get pregnant for a couple of years. Like me, she had endometriosis. Tiff had an outpatient surgery by a specialist to remove her endometriosis after I had returned home from rehabilitation.

Two months later, Tiff was pregnant. We all rejoiced at this future miracle baby whose due date was to be one day before her birthday. In hindsight, she realized that God's timeline superseded theirs. They waited patiently for their first child because our Sovereign God had prepared her instead for someone else. Someone who needed her nurturing and skill base more—her own Mama! But what a blessing when Calvin Jay Washburn was born in Newport's Hoag Hospital on November 12, 2019.

HOUSING:

"Take wives and have sons and daughters; take wives for your sons, and give your daughters in marriage, that they may bear sons and daughters; multiply there, and do not decrease." Jeremiah 29:6

Vancouver, Washington. I prayed for our kids' life purposes and mates since they were in my womb. Our son David earned his Biblical Studies Degree at Multnomah School of the Bible. He married his Seattle sweetheart, Keana. They moved soon after into their first home in Vancouver. They continued to make their family memories there. They were blessed with their first baby, Jet William Zoradi, on October 12, 2017. Our first grandchild who means the world to us.

Life at that moment in time seemed so perfect. Dreams were confirmed. Passions and purposes were pursued. Our children had launched. They had both married wonderful Christian lifemates. On the roadway thus far, our lives had run quite comfortably. But, of course, unaware—nine months later—I experienced my *head-on* kidney collision.

[The family was all thrilled once again this 2020 summer when their second baby Eden Joy Zoradi was born on July 3. So close to becoming my COVID-19, birthday buddy.]

Mission Viejo, California. Tiffani and Mike W decided that particular fateful August to move into our family's Mission Viejo home. Mike and I had purchased this house right before Tiffani's birth over thirty years ago. We raised both our children to adulthood in this home. We enjoyed many happy memories. We dedicated this home with its large backyard to the Lord to use as He wished. Many church functions and family parties took place there. Tiff and Mike moved in with us to assist in my daily routines and duties during our tragedy.

But, so much more was required from the three of them after I arrived home that October. I was so thankful for all they had done. They helped me get back on my "feet" once again. Our cat, Millie, was not too thrilled, though, when Tiffani moved over their two cats to co-occupy Millie's exclusive space. Just like the "Game of Life," we had always had a cat peg in the rear of our car.

While in the final lap at rehab, I had begun to visualize my return home, excited but apprehensive. *Was I ready for this roadside restriction?* How would I shower and brush my teeth when our home only had a powder room downstairs? My contractor brother 'Pats' offered to expand our powder room to include a roll-in shower with a sit-down bench, a bidet, and a roll-under sink. Our home had a fairly roomy, three-car garage. So, my caring brother decided—at least a month before I would be coming home—

that he would bust the powder room's wall out and frame the shower into the garage.

We were given the name of a contractor whose family attended our church. My brother contacted Erik for names of his subcontractors who worked in Orange County. Brother-in-law Paul *"Pauly"* crafted a new towel/ medication/supply cabinet over the commode and wooden ramps for my early transports. Mike and I will always be highly indebted to Pats, Erik, Pauly, and subs for all they built for us during my vulnerable time at home. Thanks to ALL who met our necessary obstacles head-on. God made sure all our needs were supplied by *'faithful partners.'*

All four of our bedrooms were upstairs. Therefore—before I came home — Mike asked two of the big muscled guys from our Thrive group to swop out our king-sized bed upstairs with the family room couch downstairs. That way, after I arrived back home, I was able *(with full assistance)* to tackle everything needed for daily life. We lived downstairs that first year from October 6th to Valentine's Day. Mike and I slept, read, or watched television downstairs with a privacy screen, while Tiffani and her Mike had their private suite upstairs. We all shared the kitchen and backyard.

Tiff helped me with my physical and occupational needs from day one at home. I had lived in four hospitals and a rehab center for almost 93 days. I was ready to be released from the hospital straight from rehabilitation. Tiffani chose many physical exercises designed specifically for me to execute from my bed. My core strength was nonexistent. It was still impossible for me to turn on my side or sit up unassisted. I needed to regain enough core muscles to scoot across a slide board to get in and out of my bed, wheelchair, shower chair, and car. Mike's brother and sister-in-law, Mark and Cathy, stepped up big to accelerate my occupational and physical help as well. I am extremely grateful for their love, support, and compassion.

Tiffani and I worked together for many days and months after returning home to our 1971 two-story Mission Viejo home. Tiff and Mike stayed with us until I was stabilized and back on an easier path to recovery. They did not move out for an entire year because they helped Mike and me during the most challenging times I encountered at home. Mike did not want to make a quick decision of retirement quite yet either. So, he asked God to show him (*with a 2x4 over his head*) when it was His perfect timing.

Laguna Niguel, California. That 2x4 obviously manifested itself in May when Tiff told us—90 day notice—they were to move out in late July to get prepared for Baby Cal. God truly blessed us with their service. We were so thankful for all their assistance. An entire year they granted to us for my recovery and therapy. That last summer at home together, Tiffani and I made a list of many tasks I needed to accomplish before Mike and I became empty-nesters once again.

After Mike spent countless hours getting rid of 32 years of "junk," we were set to move to our single-story home closer to the beach. A 55 and older, much quieter community was a Godsend. We have lived now in Laguna Niguel for a little over one year. I can *walk* throughout our entire home unassisted. We thoroughly enjoy living here. Pleasant ocean breezes flow through our house to cool me off from these stuffy, overheated prosthetics.

DREAM VACATIONS:

"And he *[Jesus]* said to them, 'Come away by yourselves to a desolate place, and rest a while.' For many were coming and going, and they had no leisure even to eat." Mark 6:31.

Pre-kids, Mike and I spent our anniversaries in several extraordinary places. Our first 1/2-year anniversary was spent at Waikiki on the island of Oahu. While somewhat strapped for cash, we stayed three blocks from the beach. We splurged though on a dinner cruise. Other anniversaries we traveled to Aspen and Whistler, BC.

Since Mike traveled some for business, we would take advantage of a *Southwest Companion Pass®□* for me so my flight would be free. Business trips took us to many excursions around the USA, Hawaiian Islands, Caribbean Islands of St.John and St.Lucia. Anywhere with SUN & WARMTH. NO teaching. NO kids. Hence the nickname *"Summer Vicki."* But, we celebrated several anniversaries in South Lake Tahoe since we honeymooned there. Often we commemorated this milestone in Northern California, as the kids wanted to be dropped off in Sacramento to stay with their cousins.

Kids came with us during the summer months for our one-week family vacations. When they got to be seven and three, Disney World and Epcot Center seemed the perfect fit. We had many kid vacations—*usually Hawaii*—over the years. As high school graduates, both our children went on mission trips as Youth With A Mission—*YWAM*—students to Cambodia.

Mike and I had never traveled over the pond. Therefore, when our Compass Bible Church offered a summer Israel trip, we quickly signed up. The Holy Land was definitely on our *"bucket list."* We jumped at our chance to travel there from late June (teaching year completed) to July 5th.

A trip of our lifetime!

I celebrated my 59th birthday at Golgotha (The Skull) at Calvary and The Garden Tomb. A fantastic vacation that made The Holy Bible come alive. This birthday concluded with *'Happy Birthday'* sung by everyone in the Tele Viv Airport terminal. I can't picture my extreme health scare if it happened one year earlier in Jerusalem. Or worse, I was found dead on an eleven-hour plane trip overseas. Zero family members able to uphold us through our frightful, life-altered event would have added untold stress to the tragedy.

PITFALLS:

"But understand this, that in the last days there will come times of difficulty." 2 Timothy 3:1

We saw another providential plan of God about 3 to 6 months before that fateful July and August of ICU. Mike had terrible, gut-wrenching thoughts. Tragic "death" episodes of some sort. In a few of these mind games, I had even passed away. *Why? Those were so frightening.* At first, Mike just dismissed it as Satan who messed with him during his prayer time lunch walks. Or possibly to upset his spiritual journey. He had never shared these terror-induced premonitions with me or anyone else.

But as we recently referred back and had time to contemplate and reflect, I told Mike that I believed God prepared his mind to accept the fact that I may die. Mike was stunned when doctors told him that my situation was life-threatening. But this prior *"death thinking"* also allowed Mike to jump into action with prayers, communication with family and friends, and medical decisions he made within seconds after we returned to the ER. We concluded that Mike was allowed to process that information beforehand because God had prepared him for battle during his wife's survival.

On May 26th—our 39th anniversary at the time—we celebrated at the cabin for the long Memorial Day weekend. It was just over one month before my 'kidney shutdown' episode. We discussed how blessed we had been our whole lives. We accepted God's gift of salvation early on in our lives, so I knew we trusted God in all situations. Sure there were ups and downs as those three miscarriages, a move from Sacramento to Orange County away from extended family, and those long commutes every day for Mike.

But, the 1992 death of our beloved sixteen-year-old nephew—Justin William *"Trustworthy"* Patterson—had shaken our family's faith like no other situation. Justin's untimely, unexpected car accident the very day he received his driver's license was by far THE MOST tragic event of our lives. If given a choice from God, I would have chosen to experience my

81

loss of limbs rather than to have lost this precious young man—a young soul for Jesus.

Justin was on his way home from their church's Wednesday evening youth group meeting. His Christian girlfriend was in the front seat next to him while his best friend stretched across the back seat. All three were headed back from town. He was the only teen in the car that evening who did not survive. Death date: July 8th, 1992.

On the anniversary of Justin's death—26 years later—my brother (Justin's father) confirmed to my husband, "Vicki is NOT dying today!" God spared my family *"sorrow upon sorrow" [Phil. 2:27]* if I had passed on that exact anniversary date of a prior family tragedy.

Therefore, after 39 years, we reflected on God's goodness and faithfulness. The numerous blessings, along with all the trials that we had experienced so far in marriage, were confirmed. I challenged Mike with this question, "Do you think we would stand firm in our faith if we were in a fox hole situation?" His answer was similar to what I would have answered. "I believe so, but we won't know until we are tested...*tested by fire.*" Little did we know that anniversary weekend that we **would** find ourselves—just eleven days later—in that *"fox hole"* being excessively tested almost unto death!

TRANSPORTATION:

I had always had fears of being FORWARD & BOLD—a covert op—in my witness for Jesus Christ before my trial. I was always God's ambassador when the subject came up. I attempted to drive my conversations toward God and faith. But, *'off the get-go'* wondered how best to get the conversation to roll in the first place smoothly. It reminded me of when I learned to drive my first stick shift.

MERCY, that was a disaster!

82

That poor car lurched, jumped, shook until I either reengaged the clutch or gave it a little more gas. I was ultra embarrassed—multiple stall outs. As a new high school driver, I had tried to learn on my parents' new 1974 Chevy Vega Hatchback's unforgiving clutch. As a high school junior, a friend had spent one-on-one time as he taught and instructed me on the gear shifts from first to second. I became efficiently comfortable with my first owned vehicle—a silver 1968 Datson 2000 Roadster Convertible. It had a black, removable hardtop with T-Bird-Esque emblems. Obviously, I am a car enthusiast.

About the same time, Mike had his death thoughts of me, and my thoughts were that I should start to work on my gospel boldness as a Jesus witness. I went door-to-door with our *Evangelism Explosion (EE) Team* at church. Mike had ramped up to share his faith this way a year or two before I joined the group. He went out Saturday mornings while I took countless hours to grade all my weekly Friday exams.

When I joined the team, we knocked on doors and invited people to go to church. We talked about their beliefs, followed suit, shared our faith, and the biblical gospel message. Mike noticed that we had a much better success rate of open doors and opportunities when a woman stood on the other side of the door.

This experience truly helped prepare me to tell my story and share the Gospel's "Good News" with others. God adjusted my courage which added more layers of readiness than I needed three months before my illness. Just like the clutch and stick shift, when I shared the Gospel of Jesus Christ, all it took was practice. The more practice, the easier and more comfortable it became. I always enjoyed owning a car with a manual transmission.

God was my Head Mechanic those months when my mode of transportation was in the ICU's repair shop. My body, engine, transmission, and inner-most parts were all up on the lift. They each were repaired by a God who is always in control. He got right to His miraculous work when doctors had given up any hope of my survival.

I have not attempted to drive since July of 2018, except for a golf cart. I haven't felt the need to drive because God took away my desire. Mike is our Highlander's chauffeur, while God is my life driver. To tell you the truth, I rather enjoy it that way.

HIGHLIGHTS:

Our 40th anniversary was spent recouping from the first of two additional kidney surgeries. I needed to have removed the 25 stones that were *still* in each kidney. God impressed upon my spirit early on that it would take a year to receive back my health. After I came home from the rehabilitation hospital's two-week visit, I trusted God for that promise. I realized on my first anniversary since amputations in September 2019; I was ready to travel. God blessed my health and mobility such that I had begun to walk by three months, robotic hands by six months, and started to write this book unassisted at twelve months.

We traveled once again to Northern California in March (six months after returning home that October). Mike and I had the pleasure of meeting Ken Tada and Joni Eareckson Tada—*through Mike's brother Mark and his wife Cathy*—at Pebble Beach. Another March weekend, we spoke to a large church audience in Lodi, Westmont's Board of Directors retreat in Santa Barbara, and various other speaking engagements twice a week. *UNTIL* the COVID-19 virus brought life to a halt.

Oh God, not another pit stop!

I took this 2020 year's early lockdown to complete, edit and publish my story. Again, God redirected our lives. I praised him for lulls in schedules and my added time to *"tune-up"* my prayer life, straighten my priorities, read more scriptures, and connect through social media with others. My four new 'tires' were balanced.

We continued to see God's providence in the trials that we faced. Mike and I continue to be in awe even today. We realized that God had been faithful and answered our prayers whether his answer was "yes" or whether his response was "no." As my journey continued, everyone verified how God directed situations in just the right way according to HIS WILL, not necessarily ours.

Joni and I met in March 2019 in Pebble Beach, California

RETIREMENT:

Substitutes were hired and taught in my place for approximately 270 days. Insurance paid out millions of dollars for my surgeries, prosthetics, and recoveries. I wholeheartedly exclaimed, "I am one who is extremely blessed." I cannot help but wonder if that was an additional reason God directed me into the teaching profession.

A few months before Mike's retirement, while I was still a teacher on leave, we traveled back to our family cabin once again. All of my relatives wondered if I would be emotionally fit to face that problematic hurdle. I walked back in through the front door after smelling those familiar pines. I heard the rushing water once again. As I checked out the friendly cabin, I stood at the kitchen's 1950 metal sink, turned back towards Mike, as tears streamed down my face. He held me tenderly and allowed valuable time for us both to grieve the loss of my hands and feet. About three to five minutes later, I felt released from that heavy physical burden. I once again fell more in love with our cabin, its beautiful surroundings, and my amazing husband. God knew that I would need and highly value this private getaway place roughly ten years after the deed was signed.

Before I officially ended my teaching career, Mike had retired in the summer of 2019 after he had worked thirty years at Medcom, Inc. I had well over one hundred sick days, vacation, and holiday pay that led to my retirement on January 17th, 2020—even though I had not worked a day past mid-June of 2018.

Mike and I had spoken to many people via groups from 20 to 300+ crowds—Bible study groups, worship services, keynote speakers at spiritual events, and radio interviews. We told others of God's incredible miracle. Also, we had the privilege to share how God used our platform to reach many with the gospel message of Jesus Christ. We made ourselves available to God for however He chose to lead us. Mike and I have incredible opportunities now and in the future because God purposely planned our steps ever so long ago.

I cruise back once again to my former hospital's fiery trials eight weeks before all four amputations. God granted His Peace through testing. And rest was allowed through trauma. Follow me back again to Marshall Hospital, where all this tragedy had begun...

BUT GOD...

"But you, O Lord, are a God merciful and gracious, slow to anger and abounding in steadfast love and faithfulness." Psalm 86:15

Empty-Nesters

6 Weeks Before Major Illness
Celebrating with Mike's Sister Yvonne and Tiffani

CHAPTER 4

PEACE, SWEET PEACE

"I have said these things to you, that in me [Jesus] you may have peace. In the world you will have tribulation. But take heart; I have overcome the world." John 16:33

As I laid in my ICU bed, the last memory I had in Marshall Hospital was confusion. I had no idea what my mind and body had gone through. I possessed zero comprehension of the severity. I admit, I received no clue that I had been terribly close to death. I believed that soon I would be released from the hospital and headed back to our vacation cabin in the woods.

Mike informed me that my physicians in Placerville had quickly begun to administer my first two blood pressure vasopressor drugs. These medications were imperative for my survival. Right away, as I was barely conscious and never recalled, I asked him and Tiffani to please rub my feet. They tingled, throbbed, and were pretty painful. The blood pressure meds kept the blood flowing around my core which helped my damaged organs from failing. Although, my limbs' blood circulation was drained.

Soon, I no longer talked because of my ventilator but wished to communicate with Mike, Tiff, and Mike W, who stayed with me in my dark, chaotic ICU room at 2 am. With no other means of communication, I began to "show" my words through some rudimentary sign language. In recollection, I signed, *'I love you.' 'Drive me outta here!' 'Let's Go'*... I didn't know if they knew what I tried to convey.

Mike realized I wished to leave, so he bent over my bed and gently whispered right into my face, "Honey, I know you want to leave, but we can't go just yet. You are a VERY sick girl. The doctors and nurses are here to help you. You need to fight. Please fight. I love you so much!" These three knew that I wanted to speak but couldn't. So, Tiffani handed me a scrap of paper with a pen. I guess I wrote several yellow sticky notes, of which I don't recall that I wrote. I wish Tiff had thought to keep these memory notes.

But—within the hour—it did not matter. I had lost consciousness once again.

Marshall Hospital was not equipped for the continuous dialysis that I required, so I was transported by ambulance to Sutter Memorial in Sacramento after my second overnight. That facility touts a 62-bed ICU unit that could do more for my chance of survival than the smaller community hospital. Medical staff informed Mike that I would die if I stayed. But on the flip side, the unknown risk was I may arrive DOA *(Dead On Arrival)* if transferred. "If Vicki positively WILL die, no doubt, if she stays, then let's transfer her," Mike decided. One fact remained, I barely survived that noontime transport.

The circuit of Marshall was completed.
Onward to the next race—Sutter Memorial Hospital

~*~

Prayers were the only route my family used during my first two weeks of critical care. All my loved ones concluded only through God could severe medical negatives turn to positives. I had always been considered *'touch and go'* from hour ONE. Here are two words pressed heavily at this juncture: TEARS and PRAYERS.

Our many loved ones who supported our family at Sutter Memorial, out-of-town family members, our church family, friends, school colleagues, and many others had been lifting me to God in their prayers. The attending physician notified Mike that Monday evening, there was nothing else medically they could do for me. I had received their arsenal—5 strong vasopressors—which attempted to bring my blood pressure up to a minimum. Or for my BP to register something, *anything*, on the monitor. All five were at maximum dosage! One was epinephrine for many days.

Just the thought of epinephrine—Adrenaline—at total dosage was a fright for my family. When I heard my story later from Mike, it brought back a television memory. It warned of the time when I watched a particular medical series where...

Hollywood Doctor—stabbed a patient with a humongous syringe full of epinephrine...

straight into their patient's heart...

The patient began to gasp...

sucked in as much air into their lungs as humanly possible...

immediately shot upright in their hospital bed...

eyes wide open and dilated...

forever to live again!

I don't recall my scene quite so dramatic, but this pretty much portrayed the situation. Except, I was on epinephrine at max dosage for five days.

My predicament became direr and direr as minutes, hours, and eventually, days progressed. Mike prayed, *"God, if you are waiting to heal Vicki, everyone will KNOW that You are a God of miracles and healing. Even now, it is not too late."* But God delayed even longer...

91

Not yet. Wait. Patience.

In the Bible passage of John 11, Jesus postponed his journey for **two** days before He fulfilled the raising of Lazarus from the dead. By the time Jesus arrived, Lazarus had been dead **four** days.

"But when Jesus heard it he said, 'This illness does not lead to death. It is for the glory of God, so that the Son of God may be glorified through it.' Now Jesus loved Martha and her sister and Lazarus. So, when he heard that Lazarus was ill, he stayed **two days longer** in the place where he was." (*John 11:4-5*)

"Martha said to Jesus, 'Lord, if you had been here, my brother would not have died. But even now I know that whatever you ask from God, God will give you.' Jesus said to her, 'Your brother will rise again.' Martha said to him, 'I know that he will rise again in the resurrection on the last day.' Jesus said to her, 'I am the resurrection and the life. Whoever believes in me, though he die, yet shall he live, and everyone who lives and believes in me shall never die. Do you believe this?' She said to him, 'Yes, Lord; I believe that you are the Christ, the Son of God, who is coming into the world.'"(*John 11:21-27*)

All the doctors had done their absolute best for me. Not one tool remained in their toolbox that my healthcare providers had not tried and had attempted everything on my behalf. I was a *'totaled vehicle'* in their top-notch, fix-it shop.

Would I ever live to race again?

The head nurse put down in my chart that morning that I would code on Monday night, July 9th, around 10 pm. They questioned Mike if he wished for any heroics when I coded. His answer was quick and decisive, "Absolutely Yes. Whatever it takes." So the head nurse placed the crash cart within view just outside my room. All the hospital staff exited with downcast faces. It became family time.

Mike voiced to all my supporters still in the family waiting room, "We have prayed our hearts out to God for three days. God is no less God if He heals Vicki or He chooses to take her home to heaven. If you are with me, follow me into Vicki's room." They all followed.

Mike stood behind me at the head of my bed. David and Tiffani also were located close to support both their mom and dad. David and Mike stood on my right while Tiffani was on my left. The rest of my family formed a wide semi-circle around the foot of my bed. They were all crammed in amongst my various monitors. *"Packed in"* as if they were my college suitemates who all squeezed tightly into a borrowed Volkswagen Bug for a Santa Barbara beach day.

I was surely dying at this point. I had no recollection at the time, except I sensed that the area around me was full of people. They sang my favorite hymns I had learned in Sunday school—Great Is Thy Faithfulness, How Great Thou Art, It Is Well With My Soul. I literally heard them as they sang beautifully in four-part harmonies. I sang out silently in my soul my *'tenor notes'* in harmony.

Certainly bizarre. Deeply curious.

The reason did not compute how I *'saw'* my nephew Ryan with his phone out. Had he viewed lyrics? Or perhaps took pictures? I'm not quite sure how I witnessed all this, on account that Tiffani told me later that she asked the nurses to bandage my eyes totally shut. These eyeballs of mine had retained extra fluids, which in turn caused intense swelling and extreme bulging. A ghastly sight, I'm sure! How was that possible that I recognized or viewed anything?

Mike spoke for me while my tubes protruded starkly out of my nose, mouth, and trach. He told every present loved one—about twelve—how much they meant to me. Afterward, family members around the room voiced how much I had impacted their lives. *Very Sweet.* Each shared what was on their

93

hearts. All said their good-byes. But these *'Words of Love'* for me, I never heard. My soul heard music, but not speech.

Strange. I had obviously skidded into loss of consciousness once more.

Many tears were shed that day. I progressively grew worse and worse. So sad. They mournfully filed back out to the family lounge area. They waited to hear the expected news that I passed. Most figured it would not be long until I headed home to heaven to be with my Lord. I always commented that THIS world was not my home. Spiritually and physically, I was ready to go. When doctors said, "No," that's when God said, "Yes!"...

Almost immediately after everyone had filed out, Mike and my niece Michelle stayed behind in my monitor-packed ICU room. It was approximately 5 pm when the family exited. Both had just begun to talk alone together as they stood next to my bloated, comatose self. Within minutes, that's when it happened...

Michelle (*confused*) spoke up, "Uncle Mike? Aunt Vicki's monitor is registering a blood pressure." "What?" Mike turned around, and there it was. Faint. 60/30. However, it was still dangerously low. This occurrence was the first time I had reportable blood pressure in about half a day. He ran to snag a nurse to have her explain. "Could this be accurate?" Mike questioned my nurse. She expressed that the machine would not put out a false reading. She left to inform my doctor that I indeed had blood pressure. Extremely low, but one nonetheless.

"Vicki has blood pressure! God has raised her BP!" Mike excitedly declared as he quickly ran into the Family Lounge. They collectively were shocked, and some rushed back in to see me. They all praised God for this glimmer of hope.

Our family was quite Amazed—Bewildered—Confused—Dazed.

My blood pressure had remained dangerously low without a reported readout for eleven+ hours. "Vicki's not out of the woods yet," professionals warned. I still produced an undetectable heartbeat. David stayed in ICU overnight that Monday with his dad to give Tiff and Mike W a well-deserved break. They took turns as they checked in on me and rested throughout the night. Mike advised David and the medical staff, "Wake me if ANYTHING changes, good or bad."

MIRACLE TUESDAY!

At four o'clock in the morning, my shallow blood pressure instantly—**miraculously**—rose to a normal range of 120/60. So, David woke up his father. This realization was truly a miraculous event! God divinely stepped in. He alone chose to heal me. My Creator had not appointed me unto death. July 10th's MIRACLE happened only after a Monday full of heartache and devastating news for my family.

Doctors stood in stunned disbelief. My blood pressure was normal. *What*? One would have thought I had returned from the dead. But, no—I had remained with them. The hospital staff was baffled, puzzled, astounded. *Really*? Any reasons otherwise were unfounded. All praise belonged to God. The family was ecstatic. I must, therefore, still wait patiently for my heavenly dwelling place and resurrected body.

God's healing hand showed mercy toward my family and me. I surmised He had more for me yet to accomplish here on earth. God's glory was seen and felt throughout the hospital that day. I wished I would have been conscious enough to appreciate what the Lord had done for me at that exact moment in time. He answered the prayers of my family, friends, and folks from church.

I was not completely healed that July 10th day. I would need more surgeries and prayers along this treacherous road of illness. My liver had a clot and was still failing. My kidneys had all but shut down. Heart pumped at 20 percent capacity. Fluids filled my lungs as extra liquids—18 liters—

insulated me. Lactic acid was at 6.75, but to sustain life, it should be no lower than 7.0. I resembled the great image of 'The Michelin Man' [1].

BUT GOD...

...in His infinite wisdom and power, eventually healed all of my organs in His perfect time. Atheist physicians, who were involved in my case, produced no explanation regarding this phenomenon. Had they fully witnessed a front-row seat to a miracle? Logically, scientifically, none of this made any sense. One of these atheistic physicians confessed to Mike, "Well, your family sure has something special. I see the strong bond and faith you have with your God." It made total sense to my faith-filled family. They all prayed, and God answered on my behalf.

Most family members had left earlier to their homes to eat dinner and rest for the night. A handful apprehensively answered the call from Mike in the wee hours of the morning. It was my beloved spouse who called excitedly and explained my miracle. His bride of 39 years had survived the night. He shared that my blood pressure was up to a normal range. Many thought Mike phoned to inform them that I was "*gone*." Blessed be the name of the Lord. All were in awe. As if God had announced...

"Okay, stand back. Watch and witness MY POWER at work!"

It again took my memory back to Exodus where the LORD spoke directly to Pharaoh through Moses..."But for this purpose I have raised you up, to show you my power, so that my name may be proclaimed in all the earth." Exodus 9:16

My fifth and final vasopressor was experimental. The pharmaceutical company wanted us to give a "*glowing testimonial*" that their medication had saved my life. Once Mike and I told them that we would give credit to our God who saved me, they declined to talk to us further. It was God who revealed His will at my most critical hour. He was in the driver's seat, not these well-educated, experienced doctors, organ specialists, ICU physicians, trauma surgeons, nurses, orderlies, or hospital staff. GOD was in control, not man.

I never had an *'out-of-body'* feeling or experience like some people claim who are close to death. I took comfort in the fact that once a true believer in Jesus Christ dies, their soul is immediately with the Lord.

After *"Miracle Tuesday,"* I was taken out of my induced coma on about the tenth day. Mike wanted me to hear just how God miraculously had spared my life. This information he shared soothed my entire being—Peace, sweet peace. God was active and held me safely in His mighty arms of love. I still was not verbally communicating because of my ventilator. To be transparent, I was *STILL EXTREMELY ILL.*

When my gentle, awestruck husband informed me what happened, he asked if I had experienced something supernatural from God as well. *Boy, I sure did!* I nodded my head up and down "yes." I had experienced a gift from God. It was like a vision, even when my eyes were swollen and bandaged shut. I couldn't wait until the day I could contribute to the conversation and share the marvelous episode from my perspective.

~*~

I peacefully prayed alone, often in the quietness of my quarters. While in ICU—from all of my hospital beds—I focused my eyes on the highest visual point possible in each room. Usually, that was straight ahead where a wall met the ceiling. I am not sure exactly which hour I witnessed this scene, but I believed it was when my family was in earnest prayer for me in the Family Lounge. I do not recollect anyone in my room at the time. Here is how I explained this scene after I could eventually talk and share.

I prayed to God—*when conscious*—like I usually did at home. Before this devastating sickness, I experienced mornings of prayerful worship as I got ready for work. Prayers on the run throughout the day. Bible reading and prayer time each evening in my steamy bath and focused conversations in bed after I retired for the night. Still, in ICU, I was filled with sweetly calmed peace even though I was paralyzed, unable to move any muscle. I questioned my circumstances.

Why can't I shift over, lift my pinky, or turn my head? I am totally immobile! Why? How did I get this way?

As I began in my mind to ask God for answers, I looked up across to the wall/ceiling in front of me and saw a moving tower of angels. Floor to ceiling. While not astonished to see them, I thought to myself and wondered at the time.

Why are these angelic beings not surrounding my bed? Are they here to usher me to heaven? No, they are not ministering to me at all. So, why are they here? What are they doing?

I continued to watch them intently. Peacefully. I noticed that these 'guardians'—three in particular—were between my ICU room and the Family Lounge next door. *(My room was the closest room to the nurses' station because I was the most critical.)* They possessed angel forms, but I saw through them. The most comparative description I explained later was: Each angel was iridescent and colorful—as see-through as bubbles in the sunshine.

I believed this scene was given only to me at the time. Not meant for others. The heavenly angel on top of the pillar appeared profoundly strong. He continually wielded a giant, double-bladed sword and encircled it well above his head. Very intense! He was keenly engaged in battle. My mind questioned once more.

Is he warding off death? Could this be Spiritual Warfare? Is he sent to protect me?

I was not privy to what Mike, my kids, and other family members were doing at this point. Was this when they were fervently in prayer on my behalf? I still, to this day, do not know. Later by those present next door, I was told that they had never experienced such a unified, Spirit-filled, heartfelt outpouring of petitions to God. Their wife, mother, sister, daughter, aunt, or niece was dying and needed divine intervention.

Two other angelic beings further down the tower petitioned to God for me through the Holy Spirit. I heard nothing audible, but I sensed that they uttered words of prayers from the saints.

Scripture corroborates,

"Likewise, the Spirit helps us in our weakness. For we do not know what to pray for as we ought, but the Spirit himself intercedes for us with groanings too deep for words. And he who searches hearts knows what is the mind of the Spirit, because the Spirit intercedes for the saints according to the will of God. And we know that for those who love God all things work together for good, for those who are called according to his purpose." Romans 8:26-27

I wanted to make sure that I hadn't been just delirious from all my medications. So a full year later—*like an excellent biblical student*—I began to search the scriptures. I found this example: In Prophet Elisha's day, he called on the One True God of Israel for deliverance. Angels were sent to help defeat their Syrian enemies in 2 Kings 6...

"When the servant of the man of God [Elisha] rose early in the morning and went out, behold, an army with horses and chariots was all around the city. And the servant said, 'Alas, my master! What shall we do?' He said, 'Do not be afraid, for those who are with us are more than those who are with them.' Then Elisha prayed and said, 'O LORD, please open his eyes that he may see.' So the LORD opened the eyes of the young man, and he saw, and behold, the mountain was full of horses and chariots of fire all around Elisha."

I was taught very young about the Bible story of angels who moved up and down Jacob's ladder. Whether I had dreamt of these angels or saw a vision of angels, I am not sure. But, either way, I had passed through this first 'tunnel of fire' trial. I was *"Tested by Fire"* like many others who had come before me. Much like the famous American motorcycle stunt performer Evel Knievel [2], my vehicle continued to barrel through even more flames. More fire. More *"testing."* My road ahead came into view with many steep, fiery curves, engulfed corkscrews, and flamed straightaways yet to be experienced. God had saved my life, and I was so grateful. Thanks be to God for my life miracle. He was with me through it all.

Those first two vasopressors caused my feet to tingle painfully early on. But, I never actually felt further pain during this two-week testing period. I had been peacefully sedated. There was one exception. When my respirator produced a choking/drowning feeling, the hospital staff informed Mike that I would encounter no other discomfort. That was true. I hadn't. Unless maybe the pain was concealed so profoundly in the recesses of my mind. Computed pain was non-existent until much later.

Peace, comforting peace.

I knew of God's sweet peace during those precious nightly moments with my Lord in prayer. I treasured His tremendous peace and tranquility throughout my delays at all four hospitals. But sure, there were times of panic when my call button became dislodged, unable to receive nurses' assistance. Absolutely, I cried hysterically when my upper body slumped over the side of my bedrail and—due to massive loss of strength—my face planted sideways into my fallen pillow. Of course, I was too weakened to sit up properly, and sometimes, at night, no one came immediately to my rescue. This situation made labored breathing even more frightening.

Every two hours throughout my many care facilities, nurses or CNAs changed my position with extra pillows, preventing bedsores. My mouth and throat, extremely parched from medications, constantly sought hand-fed ice chips that relieved my anguish. Electric fans kept me semi-cool when circulated blood no longer reached my extremities.

I had countless surgeries performed for an entire month while in the ICU in Sacramento *(the city of my birth)*...

- First, a nasogastric tube insertion down my nasal passage.

- More stent surgeries that bypassed that darn kidney stone.

- A port under my skin directly down from my clavicle's right side to draw blood and distribute additional medications.

- A gastrointestinal feeding tube.

- Constant IVs in both arms.

- Two groin surgeries which found no readings of blood pressure.

- Lung drainage tubes.

- Toxic E.Coli tainted kidney tubes for continuous dialysis.

- Tracheal procedure.

- Ventilator, Scans, MRIs, chest x-rays.

- Urinary catheters.

I'm confident that there were more surgeries along the way, of which I am unaware.

Other horrors transpired early on in my race for wellness and endurance. When I was delirious in ICU, horrors often loomed during my fitful sleep. Chilling fear like vivid nightmares of electrocution, false identities, entrapment, incapacitation, distrust, captivity, etc., pursued. Luckily, I had never experienced these dramatic crises of trepidation around family. Perhaps they only attacked my psyche and not my conscious thoughts.

"Sepsis shock, vasopressors, and a combo of all Vicki's medications may cause her some nightmares," a critical care staff member had advised Mike. Stark memories of these *mental tortures* all rushed back to my conscious brain much later after I had returned home from rehabilitation. I recalled these Post-Traumatic Stress Disorder flashbacks slowly—one at a time— along my first year's journey. Something had triggered my mind for remembrance. Then, I faced each memory head-on, dealt with it for a day or so through prayer, then turned it loose back to God for His counseled healing.

Finally, roughly ten days in Sutter Memorial, I cognitively awoke from my medically induced coma. I noticed that my hands and feet had turned a soft, purplish gray.

How did my limbs get unusually swollen? Was I bruised? Why can I barely move my fingers?

As a teacher, I had always attempted to gain knowledge and reasoning through questioning. I did not know then that amputations were on the horizon—a legitimate possibility.

Doppler radar revealed zero blood flow in either my hands or my feet. Mike told all my physicians and nurses, PTs and OTs, that it was *his job* as my husband to inform his wife that she may lose all four limbs. This advanced directive was added to my chart. The blood flow had not pulsed through my extremities for quite an extended time.

Mike experienced peace after crying out to God that night on his way to my brother-in-law Paul's parents' home.

[Jack and Ruby Parks just so happened to be traveling out-of-town for a long, extended vacation and kindly offered up their home to any family member who needed a place to stay. They live FIVE minutes from the hospital.]

As he cried, Mike pressed on through prayer, "God, how am I going to tell Vicki that she's going to lose her hands and feet? She uses her feet daily, but she uses her hands constantly. God, please help me." He previously requested additional prayers for restored hands and feet from all my prayer warriors. He was emotionally and physically exhausted. Moments later, his head hit the pillow. Sleep came almost immediately—only to be semi-awakened by a dream from God.

Here's the dream our God showed him.

We were walking in a grocery store together, and Vicki was pushing the cart. The checkout line had about three people ahead of us. The lady behind us noticed Vicki's hands were different. Vicki asked, "Do you want to hear my story?" When she affirmed that she did, Vicki began to tell her history of how she had lost her hands and feet and of God's miraculous healing. She then went on to tell her the gospel message of Jesus Christ.

When Mike fully awoke, he was elated. It was not about this temporal, earthly situation. But rather the peaceful eternal perspective that he was given. God showed him that I was going to be okay. We both clung to this **eternal**, God-viewed outlook. Jesus Himself looked at the everlasting reason when illness or health trials plagued people of His day.

Jesus Heals a Man Born Blind... "As he *[Jesus]* passed by, he saw a man blind from birth. And his disciples asked him, 'Rabbi, who sinned, this man or his parents, that he was born blind?' Jesus answered, 'It was not that this man sinned, or his parents, but that the works of God might be displayed on him.'" John 9:1-3

On the other hand, Mike was amply nervous once he knew then that God would not wholly heal my hands or feet. He asked my prayer warriors to continue still to pray. His spousal prayers, questions, and interests at the time included...

When should I disclose this to Vicki? What will be her mental state? I can't share too early, or she won't remember our conversation. I can't share too late, or she will begin to question her medical team.

Mike experienced such peace. The "peace that passes all understanding" as he drove to the hospital one morning to tell me this most difficult amputation news. My husband had many people still praying fervently for a resolute emotional response from me. Mike came into my ICU room after I winked at him as he walked through the doorway. He had an incredibly peaceful, though apprehensive, look on his face. "And the peace of God, which surpasses all understanding, will guard your hearts and your minds in Christ Jesus." Philippians 4:7

After much prayer, counsel, and assurance by God, he gingerly told me medically what had happened—why my hands and feet had turned gray. He also gently disclosed that amputations were probable unless a first-century miracle occurred. Amputations, I realized then, were inevitable unless the hand of the Almighty reached out and healed me once again. Except, I noticed by that day, my hands and feet had gotten much, much worse.

I think God had prepared my heart. Deep down inside, after I looked at my blackened "mummy hands" and my booted, coal-black "wrinkled feet," I knew Mike had spoken truth. We never did sugarcoat things with each other. I trusted that what he had rehearsed was true. This was my response..."God healed my body and kept me from dying, which is my miracle. Losing my hands and feet will become my ministry."

"...For flesh and blood have not revealed this to you, but my Father who is in heaven," Mike instantly quoted to me from Matthew 16:17.

I immediately felt the peace that we both knew could only have been granted from Above.

~*~

I lived in ICU for 35 days—July 6th through August 10th. Mike somehow needed to get me back to Southern California. A nurse sought him out on one of her shifts. "Just get Vicki home!" she implored. *How?* I was still so critical and vulnerable. Mike attempted to find a hospital in Southern California that would take such a fragile patient. Tiffani finally secured a facility that would take that risk—Kindred Hospital in Westminster. My transfer was arranged through our insurance company Blue Shield of California.

Yay! I soon would be only 25 miles from home rather than 433.

On a Friday morning, intensive care staff mildly sedated me for the long, vivid, 8-hour ambulance ride to Kindred. We drove I-5 South through August's stifling heat of 104° that particular summer day. Smoke from the recent California wildfires penetrated the air. I named this route *"HELL'S HIGHWAY."*

Three attendants accompanied me—driver, alternate driver, and an attendant in back with me. Mike followed behind the ambulance in our 2016 Toyota Highlander. Since my gurney faced backward, I often noticed (between naps) Mike's anxious face. He smiled and waved to me quite often. Sometimes he even blew me kisses. Unfortunately, as I laid prone, I was buckled and belted and could not reciprocate. At first, I experienced the sensation of being rocked around too much in the rear of the ambulance. So, I asked the attendant early to please "cinch" all my seat belts tighter. I was afraid I would get carsick, or rather, ambulance-sick. Praise God. I didn't. That tighter cinch helped my stability. My thoughts of God, my Protector, relaxed me.

I slept. I prayed. I talked. I remember distinctly, I prayed soulfully and worshipped the names of God entirely during my long traveled freeway ride. This act calmed my mind and spirit. It provided for me a relaxing, most peaceful journey.

'You, God, are my Rock, my Fortress, my Protector, my Redeemer—Jehovah, The Great I Am, Elohim, Creator...' and many, many more.

After I had contemplated and praised each name, I peacefully drifted back off to sleep.

Rest, peaceful rest.

~*~

We stopped only once off junction Hwy 41 on Interstate 5 for lunch, a stretch, and fuel fill-up. HOT! High temps were triple digits. Alternate driver *'Shotgun'* went and grabbed food. I stayed put, buckled in the back. *Where else would I go? Roll with him into McDonalds? Ha!* No Happy Meal or soda for me. I was not allowed to eat solid foods just yet. The driver refueled our ride as the attendant talked with me.

In the meantime, Mike came over and checked on my progress and comfort. When he opened the back door of the ambulance, a hot wind whipped inside. This hot blast felt as if my curious husband had opened the front, blazingly heated hood instead. At the exact moment, one pleasant smell of their tasty French fries accosted me. *Whoa! Double Difficulty.* It smelled delicious, I must admit. Mike traded phone numbers with my far rear companion, and they kept each other informed of my progress as we proceeded along the route.

Friday rush hour Los Angeles traffic. Need I say more? I asked our driver point-blank why he had not run the siren to *'speed'* things up a bit. Shotgun alternate replied, "Number One, you are not an infant. Number Two, you are not in a lifesaving situation anymore. And Number Three, the freeway lanes are super packed, bumper to bumper, with vehicles crammed together. So no, sorry, I can't." *What a drag!...*literally.

But his statement gave me peace, ease, and comfort. None of these three medical professionals thought I was too fragile. *Hallelujah!* Unfortunately, it didn't help with my anticipation or my trepidation. So off to Kindred Hospital, we traveled at a terribly slow, pokey pace.

The ambulance eventually pulled into Kindred Hospital's parking lot by early evening. I was delighted to spy many helium balloons and flowers held by our loving daughter Tiffani and our caring son-in-love Mike W. My husband had pulled in directly behind us. Everyone was pleased we arrived safely after this agonizing, forever-long trip. That included me because I was that much closer to home.

I felt full of gratitude yet a twinge of sadness for my companions. After they stopped for half an hour to stretch and eat dinner, these three immediately had an eight-hour journey back to Sacramento THAT SAME FRIDAY EVENING! The irony of it all? I was back with my loved ones while they were still hundreds of miles away from theirs.

Mike spent the night with me that night in my private room. He promised to stay with me for any new change in locations. God had brought me to Kindred Hospital for less than a two-week stay. I had always wondered, *"Why here, God, why here?"* The Great I Am, in His sovereignty, had me wait patiently at this quick rest stop. Kindred was the exact place where God prearranged a group of highly experienced *'bodywork crew'*—my surgical amputation team. I needed these expert surgeons before I arrived in Long Beach. God again had gone before me and had pre-mapped out my itinerary. He chose my main doctor at Kindred Hospital *'Doctor E. Ficient'* who assembled this amazing, highly sought, experienced squad. They had a combined 100+ years of medical expertise.

On the road again...

August 20th, I was transferred by ambulance for the third time to my fourth hospital—Long Beach Memorial. My team of surgeons practiced medicine on the 4th floor's Wound Care Unit. Since my extremities were damaged from dry gangrene, they all were given ample time to evaluate my case individually. My mummified feet *(with my cutely manicured, bright pink nail polish with white flower designs)* were in medical boots for their protection. Necrotic (*decayed*) toes had been known to fall off, break, or snap inside their bandages. Gross. Luckily, this was not the case for mine.

Both hands were all bandaged up with white gauze. Right-hand fingernails looked like little pink tires on Barbie's first pink 1962 Austin Healy roadster. While my left hand appeared identical, this dead hand resembled Barbie's 1970s American version of her Chevrolet Corvette instead. Still pink, of course! All eight fingernails (no thumbnails showed) peaked outside just like the open roofs of this doll's prized convertibles [3]. These tiny extremities were tightly nestled together, all snuggled inside their white car covers.

I was very hopeful, along with Mike, that something could be done in the bariatric pressure oxygen chamber. Could something, *anything*, possibly be executed to return blood flow or even partial blood flow to my impaired appendages? We thought of many questions to ask my specialists.

Later, after I had been settled into my new room for a few days, this co-op of doctors came in together and discussed options with us. They kicked around the idea of bariatric oxygen therapy treatment. That was the reason why I had been transferred to this facility in the first place. The specialist in charge of this treatment was present. He wanted us to try it. Kudos to him if it worked. But quickly, after they examined my unbound feet and hands, they all had realized that not much could be accomplished for that option to be viable. I just had not had enough blood flow to them for quite some time. Amputation surgery would be scheduled after demarcation occurred.

They walked out. Our hopes crumbled.

~*~

My hand surgeon *'Dr. Hand E. Man'* came back the following day and began to hold my non-bandaged left hand with his pessimistic bedside manner. The forearm down was totally black, chaffed, wrinkled, and withered. He smacked this hand somewhat hard while he stated emphatically, "THIS...IS...DEAD!" I hadn't denied that fact. I was resolute. No tears. I had not fallen emotionally apart. In fact, I appreciated his forthright honesty. It was true. My hands were dead. All four appendages were DEAD. Mike was not impressed with his abrupt demeanor. All we knew was this man who stood before us was a renowned hand surgeon from Irvine's (UCI) teaching hospital.

He confirmed that sepsis damage needed 'demarcation' anyway. He defined what that term meant: "A boundary division between damaged skin and healthy tissue." When would it stop? How much of my tissue could be saved? Could I keep my elbows which would be a substantial long-term benefit? Time alone answered all our questions. There was no rush for surgery. He left us as we pondered our concerns and expectations.

Sure, I was scared, petrified, in fact. But, I knew that God had always taken care of me my entire life. He knew my beginning, and He knew my end. I trusted God explicitly. I had given my life, my all, to Christ Jesus along with my total trust and allegiance at the tender age of eleven. I gave up control of my own life and asked Him to lead and accompany me the rest of the way. My Heavenly Father knew what I could handle. I knew that I was placed in His loving care. I put my hands in His and followed Him every step of this path. This 'life' was my new journey—my new reality. Deep down in my heart, I eventually accepted the fact that my outcome would unequivocally be amputations. All four! Which we learned was quite rare. Even still, God was faithful. He granted me His peace at the time of my suffering.

After a couple of weeks at Long Beach Memorial Hospital, surgery was finally rescheduled for September 1st. It was the long holiday Labor Day weekend. The first surgery had been postponed. After I had first arrived, I contracted another UTI, which canceled the earlier surgical date.

I attempted to convince both my foot and hand surgeons to conduct my surgeries simultaneously. My rationale to them both was, "First, I would only need to be anesthetized once. Second, the healing process and pain management could immediately begin after surgery for all four limbs. Last, I would not have an additional surgery hanging over my head a week or two later." Three great reasons, right? They reluctantly agreed. But, only after, I also advised both to get over themselves and lay aside their feelings of pride. "Put a sheet up and block each other out, if need be," I quipped, "like a c-section delivery."

God's perfect peace seen through my emotional state was incredible. How many people can sense His sweet peace during a trial such as this? The night before surgery, after everyone had prayed with me and left my hospital room for the night, I had a memorable time communing in prayer alone with God. As I mentioned, I always looked up at the ceiling, as God and I prayerfully connected each night. Later, during that fateful evening, in particular, I closed my eyes and just listened to what God's Spirit revealed to my soul.

Peace, sweet peace. A few tears trickled slowly down. Soon, I finally shared my heart and concerns with Him. I asked God reverently, "Please, LORD, I am asking once again for You to bring the lifeblood back to my hands and feet. I know even now it is not too late." I heard His gentle answer in my spirit, which was simply a soft, *"No."*

More tears welled up again. God brought to my mind all the multiple healings that He had done in the Bible. Miracles such as the man with the withered hand, the woman with the blood issue for twelve years, and the ten lepers. My caring husband, son, and son-in-law had read these accounts to me while I laid in my hospital beds night upon night. They switched off as each read these accounts for several evenings after I had regained consciousness. Maybe they had begun before consciousness. *Who knows?* These *'miracle passages'* had left a fresh imprint on my mind.

[I don't mean to quote God using words, but I don't rightly know how else to convey this conversation that took off in my silent, conscious prayer. I could feel what His Spirit was sharing with me...]

"You recall My miracles?" *[God]*

"Yes, I remember." *[me]*

"Did you ever read of them again throughout the scriptures?" *[God]*

"No. Only from different eyewitness apostles' gospel accounts." *[me]*

"Of course you didn't. But what does it say in Hebrews 11?" *[God]*

I realized that this passage of scripture included all the men of faith. Each had very trying times throughout their entire lives. Men such as Noah, Abraham, Isaac, Jacob, Joseph, and Moses. Many women of faith, also throughout the Bible—Esther, Sarah, Abigail—flooded my mind. Each one had not had an easy life. They all had suffered mightily in obedience to what God had called them to do.

His response formed in my mind, "You will be like one of these. My glory will be shown because of your trial and disabilities." *[God]*.

Tears began to stream. I sobbed, "Lord, I can't do this without Your strength." I sensed Him smile at me. He continued, "In your weakness, I Am strong. I will be your hands and feet."

Immediately, in my mind's eye, I saw a man in a tuxedo. He was at a wedding dancing with his little, fancy-dressed daughter. She was standing on his polished shoes while holding his hands. She was being led by her

"Daddy" around the dance floor. I wept some more, not out of fear, but through His comfort.

I knew right then and there that God would take care of me. He promised me that He would be my hands and feet. My limbs would not be healed. God would use my situation for *His glory*. In a way, I felt honored and privileged that God had chosen me for this difficult assignment. The Almighty had our lives under HIS control.

As Luke wrote to Christian converts..."Therefore, since we are surrounded by so great a cloud of witnesses let us also lay aside every weight, [*my dead hands and feet felt as if they were mired in blocks of cement*] and sin which clings so closely, and let us run [*I would no longer have feet*] with endurance the *race* that is set before us, looking to Jesus, the founder and perfecter of our faith, who for the joy that was set before him endured the cross, despising the shame, and is seated at the right hand of the throne of God." Hebrews 12:1-2

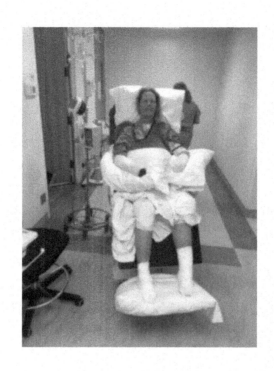

Pre-Amputations

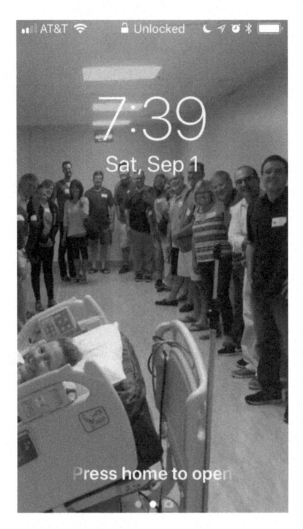

Pre-Operation Morning

Surgery was scheduled at 7:30 am—prep at 6:30—the following day. Many family members, friends, and close church people came into my room early. They spoke and encouraged me in groups of about two to four. I excitedly told them what God had shown me the night before. Not a dry eye existed. I wanted everyone to know that I was going to be okay. God was with me. God comforted me. God's peace enveloped me.

As I was being wheeled from my room on the 4th floor downstairs to surgery, it felt like twenty people lined the hallway. They smiled and threw out their words of encouragement. My cheerleaders! I felt extremely loved. The nursing staff commented that they had never before experienced such a scene. I raised my heavily weighted, tar-black, white bandaged hands like Rocky Balboa [4] as he headed into the ring to fight the fight of his life. Where else had I witnessed more than conquerors? Samson vs. The Philistines. David vs. Goliath. Or the race between *Ford v Ferrari* [5]. *Lightning McQueen* against *Strip "The King" Weathers* in the animated movie *Cars* [6].

Immediately around the corner, I had arrived at the entrance to the surgery's pre-op. As I was wheeled in, I quickly relaxed. A nurse had placed a warm blanket over me. All the nurses had done this demonstration of kindness in my hospital rooms along the way. I looked around and realized that no one had placed a heated blanket over me, except for my Heavenly Father. This act I knew was my covering of God's peace. My *'Daddy'* had tucked me into bed before surgery.

I can't explain to you how peaceful I felt. I headed into surgery to have my hands and feet removed, for Heaven's sake! I should not be so calm. I should have experienced anger, anxiety, fear, and frustration. But instead, I felt appreciation, comfort, perseverance, and steadfastness. I trusted God to take care of me. My fabulous life-mate Mike and sweet daughter Tiffani accompanied and bolstered me before surgery—much like Aaron and Hur, who held up Moses' arms in the battle against the Amalekites in Exodus 17:12. Three hours later, Mike, David, and Tiffani—my precious ones— were with me in recovery soon after surgery. I felt very supported and surrounded by those who love me most.

God's peace granted us freedom from worry or anxiety. Before any long-distance car trip, Mike always filled our vehicle's radiator with water to overflowing. He prepared our car beforehand for the possibility of overheating. In much the same way, God poured an ample supply of *'peace'* that filled our souls to overflowing before our journey ever began.

Life is our journey. The LORD prepared us long before so our engine could never overheat from our horrific testing.

God's peace flowed through us, which spread to others. Just as drips pooled under our car from an overfilled radiator, 'peace' dripped down and refreshed others around us. When family and friends witnessed that Mike and I were at peace in our tragedy, they too could rest in His promises as well.

~*~

I enjoyed driving all my vehicles ever since I turned sixteen. Nevermore so than when I cranked up *'my tunes'* while I drove. In my teens, I received or purchased from flea markets many 8-track tapes. I popped one into Mike's VW's 8-track tape player in 1977, and we sang and listened on our way to and from Westmont College. After college, we converted over to *"stereo cassette tapes"* from my purchased vinyl record albums. Over time, we graduated to CDs.

As newlyweds, Mike bought me my first brand-new piano. I enjoyed countless hours as I played and sang 70's music, Broadway numbers, Christian Rock & easy listening, and hymns. I close this chapter with one of my favorite hymns from my 47-year-old hymnal.

What A Friend We Have In Jesus

What a friend we have in Jesus—All our sins and griefs to bear
And what a privilege to carry—Everything to God in prayer

Oh, what peace we often forfeit—Oh, what needless pain we bear
All because we do not carry—Everything to God in prayer

Have we trials and temptations?—Is there trouble anywhere?
We should never be discouraged—Take it to the Lord in prayer

Can we find a friend so faithful—Who will all our sorrows share?
Jesus knows our every weakness—Take it to the Lord in prayer

Are we weak and heavy laden?—Cumbered with a load of care
Precious Savior still our refuge—Take it to the Lord in prayer

Do thy friends despise forsake thee—Take it to the Lord in prayer
In His arms He'll take and shield thee—Thou wilt find a solace there

Blessed Savior Thou hast promised—Thou wilt all our burdens bear
May we ever Lord be bringing—All to Thee in earnest prayer

Soon in glory bright unclouded—There will be no need for prayer
Rapture praise and endless worship—Will be our sweet portion there

-written by Joseph M. Scriven (1855)

as a poem to his mother in his absence [7].

"Peace I leave you; my peace I give to you. Not as the world gives do I give to you. Let not your hearts be troubled, neither let them be afraid." John 14:27

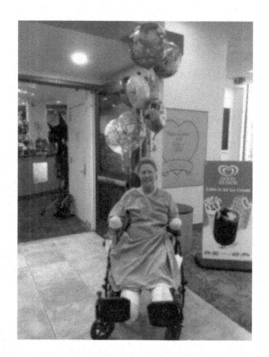

Post-Surgery—Long Beach Gift Shop—

Second Outing

BUT GOD...

"But God chose what is foolish in the world to shame the wise; God chose what is weak in the world to shame the strong;"1 Corinthians 1:27

"But for you, O LORD, do I wait; it is you, O Lord my God, who will answer." Psalm 38:15

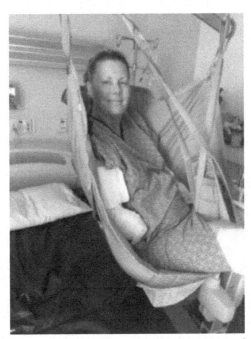

Post Amputation Rehabilitation in the Wound Care Unit
Long Beach Memorial Upstairs—4th Floor

CHAPTER 5

PUSHING THROUGH PAIN

"'Woe to me because of my hurt! My wound is grievous.' But I said, 'Truly this is an affliction, that I must bear it.'" Jeremiah 10:19

"The LORD gave, and the LORD has taken away; blessed be the name of the LORD." Job 1:21b

I never contemplated this before my amputations, but the pain comes in multiple varieties. And, likewise, different severities. Life, in general, takes twists, turns, and bends in the road that causes either discomfort or delight. These setbacks often happened in my game of life. Pain affects everyone at some point in time. There's physical pain. There's emotional pain. And yes, there is even spiritual pain.

Grief resides in the heart when you have lost someone close to you. There is that jolt of separation when someone you love hurts you deeply. Severe agony may occur if injured or internal discomfort when overly stressed. Silent pain of depression, debilitating anxiety, headaches, migraines that incapacitate all happen pretty frequently throughout society. Even toothaches cause fretful discomfort. The pain menu is endless. Multiple levels of spiritual pain may be present if lying, guilt, disobedience, even shame builds to a crescendo.

The list of various pains grows longer with each passing year of one's life. But, the anguish I never experienced before this illness was *Phantom Pain*. For sixty years, I remained clueless in regards to this unusually sporadic type of pain. But before I expose this painful torment, I must disclose my physical sufferings first.

Most of us have known physical pain. Pain happens numerous times in life from childhood, teen years, throughout adulthood, and perhaps more so when advanced in age. Countless women recall intense pain during childbirth. Or even still, different causes for painful surgeries of which many have suffered and endured. Others have lived with chronic pain continually. I pray for those individuals who must endure those agonies daily, moment by moment basis.

As a recent quadrilateral amputee, my goal is to convey my physical pain and phantom pain experiences. A "fiery journey of trials" would not be complete without full disclosure of pain and the consequences and payoffs thereof. I wondered...

Will I pass this test called pain and suffering?

I woke up from my amputation surgery extremely groggy later that afternoon. It only took my two surgeons and PA three hours to remove all four appendages and repair the remaining limbs. I remember Mike informed me that all had gone well, and my hand surgeon did save both of my elbows. My foot surgeon amputated at the perfect spot for artificial leg sockets. *Woo-Hoo!* This outcome was a victory lap. Checkered Flag waved as far as amputations were concerned. No one knew quite yet about my future prosthetics, though. I thanked the Lord right away that He had spared my elbows and knees. Such a mobility changer.

I was not in any pain. What a payoff! Doctors had amply supplied me with plenty of medications—Morphine at first. After I had slept a bit longer, I awoke to pain that I thought was quite manageable. This realization shocked me. I believed that after anesthesia had worn off, I would have been in a relatively decent amount of pain. Hours earlier, my arms and legs had been partially removed. Also, I endured internal and external sutures and multiple sturdy leg staples.

Obviously, my two physicians had prescribed for me the perfect amount. Great outcome. Although, what I didn't particularly like was the way the pain meds made me feel. Morphine equaled nausea in my wrecked body. I felt greatly nauseous. Personally, I'd somewhat have suffered an uptick in pain than nausea. The doctor in charge changed my narcotic prescription to Norco for pain management. I was very grateful. He additionally authorized some anti-nausea medication directly into my port. That helped tremendously within minutes.

The wound care staff at Long Beach Memorial was excellent. I loved all my nurses and their assistants who had my comfort in the forefront of their minds. I slowly became more alert as they cared for me physically after surgery. More settled. Less nauseated.

But, *THE MOST HORRIFIC PAIN* of all...

...was when my leg surgeon *'Dr. Do-It-Quick'* began to undress my calf wounds himself the very next morning. This procedure had happened less than ONE DAY after surgery. I was so very close to passing out from that horribly cruel pain he inflicted. Birthing two babies didn't even come a close second.

Mike realized how soon this was post operations and that I was not medicinally prepared for this intense agony. Mike commanded this elderly surgeon point-blank with authority, "STOP." This hard-headed—or hard of hearing—physician briefly paused, looked up at Mike for a fraction of a second, then kept to his task. Mike much more forcefully cried, "S T O P!"

The doctor stared at my husband with a shocked look on his challenging face and asked, "Are YOU her doctor?" And I loved *Dr. Mike's* response, "I am today!" The baffled surgeon turned and immediately left my room on the spot. "Thank you, Honey, for your loving care and concern for me." My hero and my advocate.

Later that same day, the surgeon waited while the new additional dose of pain medications had completed their job. Let me say, even then fully medicated; it was *EXCRUCIATING!* But, the doc had not seemed to notice. He continued his torture session.

That day, and once or twice a week after that, doctors began to make their rounds. To prepare for this early morning medical process, a nurse woke me up around 6 am. This healthcare worker began to unwrap all my bandages gingerly. This meeting entailed a conglomerate of about six or more health professionals. All personnel present discussed how and when their care was to be administered. Each professional discussed difficulties that may arise or those which had already occurred. Treatment ideas collaborated, even though it was evident to me who was in charge—*my older-aged foot surgeon.*

Their goals *(or next steps)* were then documented. Computer entries included best practices. Also, who was to be the designated professional to handle each procedure? Who would be notified at every crossroad? Simply put, the five Ws. *Who? What? When? Where? Why? Plus How?* The round table discussions always included the following information: pain medications, food restrictions, wound care, hygiene, physical and occupational therapies, and much, much more. Almost every employee who attended these meetings was very kind and compassionate. I was pointed in the right direction. My outcomes looked bright. With surgeries completed, I had entered the road to my recovery.

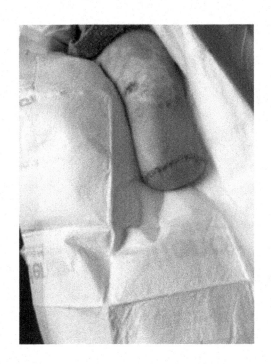

Damaged Sepsis, Burns, Sutures, and Staples

Post-Surgery—Long Beach Memorial

My hand surgeon had not even stopped by to check my wounds until late afternoon on the third day post-op. He implied that my white cell blood count would have been significantly elevated if there was an infection from surgery. It wasn't. *Thank you, God!* He always visited me later in the afternoon and alone. No nurse to aid him. No Physician's Assistant to help, unlike my other surgeon. This man undressed my hand wounds himself. He always rebandaged as well. Both surgeons assured me that my incisions had begun to heal nicely. *Doctor 'Hand' E. Man* also suggested I reach out to my prosthetist and start shrinkers (*compression socks)* on my limbs soon. Much swelling occurred after surgery. *[It took over a year before limb shrinkage had finally subsided.]*

I admired this surgeon even though he always pushed, pushed, pushed for more daily exercises. He tried to bring my arms closer and closer together with each visit. My elbows up and out to my side—just like wings on the Bat Mobile. I could not get my remaining arms closer together than about five inches apart. But he worked on that for me. He just grabbed my elbows and pressed them forward. No warning, either. Ouch, Doc. *Super Painful!* Didn't he realize that I was still recuperating? I had lost each hand, both wrists and up to the middle of my forearms. As my teaching partner, Alisa, always replied, *"O Yeesh!"*

My right arm appendage had more sepsis damage. Therefore, the residual bone was only three inches in length from the elbow down. It had required a skin wrap to save that elbow. To be honest, my whole right side had more damaged skin than my left. Who knows why? Perhaps, because the kidney stone blockage was dammed up on my right side.

I also lacked movement in both of my arms, including their range of motion. This limitation was mainly due to the five following reasons— atrophy of my muscles, all prior surgeries, necrosis, skin wraps, and amputations. I found this especially to be significant in my shoulder areas. My former hands had been as heavy as if I had attempted to lift a car's engine. I had laid totally on my back for July and August, except for rapid sponge baths, pillow props, and cleanups.

My upper extremity surgeon finally got to the point one day when he checked in on me. "Let's see if you can hold a banana between your arms today," he wondered. Those non-wrapped, exposed limbs *barely* held that fruit out in front of me. Banana wobbled. Arms shook. Stitches burned.

O-U-C-H ! But, I held on with all my strength—or lack thereof.

This proficient hand physician was not worried much about my narcotic pain meds, *but only at first.* Right after surgery, as I said, doctors prescribed morphine. That nauseous feeling subsided when they switched me to 10 mg of Norco every four hours. Then dropped the dosage to every six hours, but eventually, every eight. I was thrilled that doses were heading down, not up. But soon, my hand expert did not like that I was on *any* narcotics whatsoever. He suggested one day, "You just need to take shots of whiskey instead of pills because some of my patients have become drug addicts!"

Mike and I looked at each other in shock. *Is this a joke? Me?* A person who hates the taste of coffee is going to endure a shot of whiskey? I have never tolerated even a sip of ANY liquor—tequila, wine, beer. You name it. *Yuck!* Mike and I shared another glance and laughed. This doc did not know me very well. I'm a pharmaceutical and alcohol naïveté. I don't desire to be under the influence of any drug, much less alcohol unless ordered by a physician.

[Ten days after surgery, I was already at 25% of my first post-amputation drugs.]

The incisions—*well over thirty to forty stitches on each arm*—were unprotected during exercise. The skin on their new ends was tender, tight, and raw, like pouring salt on a fleshy wound. It was very pain-induced each time a surgeon, medical doctor, nurse, or therapist came in and checked my wounds, bandaged limbs again, rebooted, or required me to do any exercises.

But, another nice reward was that the harder I worked, the better my outcome. I had heard and bought into, *"No pains, no gains." Right?* Afterward, I looked up this phrase on the Internet. It dates as far back as the second century. People had suffered both physically and spiritually quite a bit throughout history. The first to pen these known words came from Rabbi Ben Hei Hei, who wrote, "According to the pain is the gain." Pirkei Avot 5:23 [1]. This Rabbi in the earlier century meant this as a spiritual pain if one does not obey God's commands. Spiritual gains are only acquired in obedience to God.

But, the saying was revised in the 1650 edition as a two-lined poem from Robert Herrick's *Hesperides 752:*

> "If little labour, little are our gains:
> Man's fate is according to his pains." [2]

Benjamin Franklin quoted this term, "There are no gains, without pains." in his 1734 book titled Poor Richard. He meant it as a physical fitness goal, whereas the former two penned it for spiritual growth. Franklin also had another famous quote, "God helps those who help themselves."[3] Many people think this passage is taken from the Bible, but it is not. Here is a verse in scripture regarding God's help.

"For I, the LORD your God, hold your right hand; it is I who say, 'Fear not, I am the one who helps you.'" Isaiah 41:13.

Tiffani had also worked with me post-op on my arm exercises as I reclined in my hospital bed. It was a slow process, but each day my legs and arms grew stronger. Tiff ordered 2-lb. arm weights which felt as if they were ten pounds at the time. Not much arm, leg, or core strength, I admit. I had lain prone in a hospital bed for two solid months with just enough endurance for an hour of physical therapy once a day. Sabbath rest on Sundays.

~*~

But for reference, my foot surgeon '*Dr. Quick*' suggested only after a few days post-op that I start slowly with leg exercises. "Swimmers," he called them. I wanted to scream at him and say, "You try these workouts with incisions, staples, internal and external stitches, and excruciating pain." Much like he attempted to remove my surgical wraps less than 24 hours after surgery, this doctor always suggested procedures way too early for my liking.

I was thrilled that I received my feet and both hand amputations on the same day. I had, then, a comparison of sorts between physicians, procedures, pain, and practices. What was his rush anyway? I already had to bear an extended hospital stay. Much like a long-haul trucker stuck on the side of the highway during snowy road closures. This stall out was my Long Beach mandatory pit stop for many major body repairs and a complete engine overhaul. I found all the race cars whizzed by me in their holding pattern. I waited for this 'wreck' of mine to clear.

Pink flag—Drivers, hold up while the track is cleared.
Racers, Slow Your Speed.

The day finally came for the staples to be taken out of my legs. Eight days in, the date again seemed too quick. This next time, Mike and I made sure that I had plenty of medication to counteract the unbearable pain. Luckily, it registered about a level nine (0-10) and not off the charts. I always noticed that pain radiated in my legs far worse than my arms at this juncture. This statement was true, at least for the first three months. I'm not sure why.

The staples came out slightly less painful, but I liked when his Physician's Assistant worked on me more so than the surgeon. "*Ms. PA*" *(Pain*

Alleviator) had a tender bedside manner and took patience with each step of the procedure. She walked me through whatever task she accomplished verbally. In turn, that helped me process and manage my pain much easier. Her carefree dialogue took my mind off of the process while we shared our own stories.

I got highly distressed when *'Do-It-Quick'* strongly advised my prosthetist, Rick Myers, the owner of Southern California Prosthetics, to have me up and walk before four weeks. My instant thought was, *You have got to be kidding me. Really? Well, he's the expert. What do I know about it?* Rick commented to Mike, "This doctor's timetable is highly unusual. But, I will do exactly as he ordered."

Can I tell you at week three what that experience produced? *"Ouch! Ow! Ai¡ Ai¡ Ai¡."* I stood up from my wheelchair with a plastered fake smile on my face for videos and pictures. This drama was to be a milestone, like an infant who was learning to walk. I took my first and only step. I immediately proceeded to sit right back down in my wheelchair.

I urge anyone to put themselves in my "shoes." Picture it—weakly balanced on stilts with no sensitivity except excruciating pain. No arms to hold onto the parallel bars for stability, assurance, safety, or weight distribution! Imagine further, barely three-week-old opened, raw stitched wounds fixed on the end of not one but both legs. Finally, tender amputated limbs crammed ever so tightly into each leg socket. Now walk. Grasp that scenario? It took several more weeks before I would try THAT again.

I had no idea what to expect on this troublesome stretch of road in the coming days, weeks, months, or years. Neither one of my surgeons filled me in. I realized I must not have asked enough questions, didn't recall their responses, or never wanted to know. I completely missed total comprehension until much later that I had eight severed bones, detached ligaments, and muscles, tweaked nerves, wrapped, and sewn up tightly within sepsis-damaged skin.

All these essential body components had been necessary members of this 60-year-old woman's body. "It will take twelve weeks before your severed bones will be calcified over," my absolute favorite pain/rehab physician *'Dr. Warm N. Kind-Hearted'* informed me a few months later. That took until the Christmas season of early December.

With regards to skin damage, Johns Hopkins Medicine published this information:

"People with sepsis often develop a hemorrhagic rash—a cluster of tiny blood spots that look like pinpricks in the skin. If untreated, these gradually get bigger and begin to look like fresh bruises. These bruises then join together to form larger areas of purple skin damage and discoloration." [4].

This purplish-black frostbit skin on my nose was temporary. It lasted about one month. When I looked into a mirror during weeks three and four, I resembled a puppy dog dressed up for Halloween's Fall Fest scheduled for late October. Sepsis permanently scarred the skin on my right arm and both knees.

As the sepsis infection had pulsated throughout my body in July, toxins excreted from the inside out. It was released through my skin and resembled burns. Burns began as an ultra-deep red. But gradually, they scabbed up as a dark burgundy black. My scars lightened over the months. This variant skin resembled burn scars. Some septic shock patients have skin so damaged and painful that they are no longer considered candidates for prosthetic limbs.

Friends asked me if mine continued to hurt. I informed many that my nerves are shot underneath this skin, so it's numb when touched. I am blessed, too, that my scars are hidden under my prosthetics. These scars no longer affect my performance or my mobility. Yet, I have never attempted to swim, run, bicycle, or drive. I'm sure I could try to float on a raft down our lazy river, though. *Who knows what my future holds except God alone?*

Movements in hospital beds after amputations were painfully endured as well. My legs, which were not yet healed, began to form new scars. These were slathered with salves and medicinal ointments before being rebandaged with thick wraps of gauze. At the Long Beach hospital and their rehab center, this daily process was protocol for my entire stay. My four stumps were highly protected. Cleanups, repositioned poses, straighter posture, and physical/occupational therapies put extreme stress on my fragile limbs. I am not a wimp. Tiff called me, "The Bull!"

After I arrived home and slept throughout varying intervals day and night, I was acutely aware of Mike or Tiffani's movements. Constantly, I was on high alert, ever vigilant, and ultra-protective of these vulnerable wounds of mine. More so if the slightest motion occurred.

What were some of my painful payoffs? Peace of mind for one. In the wound care unit, I heard patients who screamed, cried out in torturous agony, cursed God, and yelled obscenities at anyone and everyone. But, these individuals specifically targeted nurses. And especially in the middle of the night. The pain was revealed constantly throughout this fourth-floor trauma area. Torment seemed heightened during sunset, midnight, and wee hours of the morning. Sleep sometimes alluded us all. It was difficult to sleep through all that noise. Patients' outbursts often woke me up. Also, nurses awakened me repeatedly every two hours to monitor my vital signs.

My instant reaction as I heard these distressed and pain-soaked cries? I prayed. I sought God's comfort for those who felt anguish. I prayed that their pain and suffering might subside. Prayers to God for relieving discomfort. "Please, Father God, make Yourself known to them as You have done for me." I had many prayer warriors throughout my hospital journey. Now, I became theirs. God was my solace. He was with me as I prayed alone in my private room. Those late nights proved to produce in me the ample time of prayerful solitude, not only for my benefit but for others as well.

I began to notice that the nurses and CNAs, both male and female, came in at all hours to turn me, position me, give me meds, take my essential blood pressure, O2 saturation, and temperature. I learned fun facts about many of my caregivers during their ten- or twelve-hour shifts. I inevitably asked if they wanted to listen to my story. They knew the cause of my situation was a jammed kidney stone. That information was already in my chart. What they didn't comprehend was the severity of my near-death illness, hospital experiences, and God's miracle.

Payoff #2 during late hours? I also shared my faith in Jesus Christ during these precious nighttime regimens when staff could take more free minutes. I told them my story, and they couldn't believe that I was still alive. *Who doesn't love a great miracle story?* I shared God's goodness, faithfulness, and His healing hand. Sometimes they came into my room to 'hang out,' talk, and not be yelled at by some of their other patients. For me, these connections were highlights of being in medical confinement.

After I revealed my faith and *Miracle Story* from my heart, the next evening *(an additional benefit),* I requested them to tell me their life history and religious experiences. People were hurt in general. Others claimed loneliness. Most felt undervalued. Some seemed dejected and discouraged. In the world today, many traveled through life wearing hidden masks. We put on our happy faces and do not share with others our struggles. *"How are you?"* The answer most often is, *"I'm fine. How are you?"* Humans, I figured, camouflage our pains—Limited transparency. We don't want to expose—at all costs—our vulnerabilities.

When I permitted my hospital caregivers to speak frankly, their versions were heartbreaking and tragic. Many came from broken homes. Several 'family of origin' traumas produced deep physical, emotional, or spiritual scars. Others experienced dysfunctional families, or abandonment, abuse, divorce. Male nurses, I especially found, had mostly suffered tragedy either with their children or their spouse, or both. Divorce was rampant. Grandmas and grandpas raised their babies' babies.

Quite a few of them had never heard of the salvation granted to them by God through the blood sacrifice of Jesus Christ. Others knew about Jesus dying on the cross for their sins but asked me about repentance *(turning from sin)* and putting their total trust and faith in Him. Several caregivers thought they were "good enough" and deserved to go to heaven. A few others had already put their trust in Jesus Christ, and we talked on a deeper, more spiritual level. This time of sharing was special. Though, a small percentage didn't want to talk about this subject and let me know it. I dropped that conversation when asked.

Pain brought its captor closer to their Heavenly Father through prayer or further from God through irritating discomforts. Some deep pain made a person furious, and they turned away from Him. I found this to be valid with those I met both in and out of each hospital.

(I discuss more of my physical pain when I describe my prosthetics.)

~*~

The next stop came up fast. Green Flag had reappeared.
The Grand Marshall resumed my race...

I was moved from the 4th floor's Wound Care Unit to the bottom floor's Rehabilitation Center in mid-September. I was wheeled downstairs in my hospital bed three full weeks after amputations. I was happy to be away from the painful cries of my suitemates. I had been granted one of the more private, scenic parklike view rooms. I felt as if I were a celebrity who made her first debut on the big screen while chauffeured in a limo to the Academy Awards. Except, it was a gurney pushed by an orderly.

The rehab staff—*which still consisted of CNAs, Nurses, Tech Support, OTs and PTs, plus a Director*—were genuinely kind, caring, and funny. I nicknamed all of them right to their faces. Two CNAs I dubbed 'No-Nonsense Nancy' and 'Hilarious Hero Helen.' One nurse was 'Panic Pam' because she misplaced one of my narcotic pain meds. She began to freak out around 11 pm. After she combed through the entire room on her hands and knees in a dimly lit room with no luck, I told her to look around the sink. It was the last place I thought she had been. *Eureka!* It was found inside the top trash heap in the garbage can. I told her that I would take it anyway so she wouldn't get "written up" by her supervisor. My OT became *'Glorious Gentle Grace'* because she was extremely gentle with my hygiene needs and workouts. My two PTs were *'Painful Patrick'* and *'Merciless Monica'* even though they both were extremely kind.

We would all chuckle as I greeted each by their nickname six days a week. I didn't dole out their names lightly. The pain was felt during my bed and wheelchair transfers. Discomfort ensued whenever I moved in any direction. I could not lay down on my side and get up on my elbow unassisted. I also could not flip over from my back for *'tummy time.'* Agonized situations and soreness occurred as I learned how to get in and out of the rehab center's fake automobile. No strength. No stamina. No energy. But, with God's Spirit, YES on courage. YES on endurance. YES on fortitude. Even YES on a solid character.

Like I said, *"No pains, no gains!"*

"...but we rejoice in our sufferings, knowing that suffering produces endurance, and endurance produces character, and character produces hope, and hope does not put us to shame, because God's love has been poured into our hearts through the Holy Spirit who has been given to us." Romans 5:4-5

But then there's *Phantom Pain!*

Most folks don't feel or even understand phantom pain. I did not until I lost body parts. This form of terror had not hit me until about a month or so after amputations. The compression shrinkers on my limbs and pain medications seemed to help, but the phantom pain affected my legs the most. The odd thing about these ghost pains was that my brain registered intense pain as it radiated in the *hands and feet I no longer had.*

*Each year in the United States, between 30,000-40,000 amputations are performed (.0001% of the U.S. population). Ninety-five percent of these amputees experience residual limb pain (RLP), or phantom limb pain (PLP), or both. Residual pain is felt roughly in 68% of amputee patients. At the same time, almost 80% suffer from phantom pain in varying degrees [5].

Consequently, I still had nerve endings that "fired up" and needed to transmit somewhere. This action was their way of telling me—*their host*—they were angry and confused. My mind still believed that I had my limbs, nerves, and all. So, this particular pain felt constant and oh so 'real.' I even learned to sleep with this ongoing dilemma of vicious pain.

This phantom pain in my legs felt like someone had stomped on my toes or squeeeeezed my foot in a vice grip. Even though I knew I didn't have any toenails, joints, toes, arches, pads, bones, heels, or ankles anymore. It was such an odd sensation. The best way to describe these mysterious pains for my arms was in degrees of suffering levels.

I mean this: The lightest pain that I experienced *(levels 1-3)* felt like my hands were trapped in cement blocks—super encased and excessively heavy. I could not lift them with ease. It was exactly the same pain my "mummy hands" felt pre-amputation. That's the light, bearable pain. I have that most of the day, every day. I still do.

My brain also may produce intermediate pain signals. I share these as pins and needles *(levels 4-6)*. Pain as if my arms or legs had fallen asleep and tried to get their blood flow back once again. Sometimes, these painful sensations are more like constant palpitations, unrelenting flutters, or pain-filled pulsations.

Often, intense pain (Levels 7-8) occurred in the first three to nine months. It felt like I had been hit by a hammer, stung by a wasp, or zapped by a stung gun. My invisible hands and feet violently pulsated or throbbed. Sometimes, even currently, my phantom woes resemble as if my funny bone was smacked and nerves had gone ballistic in my elbow. It produces a sharp electric jolt—but it's not so amusing.

Even early this morning, as I laid in bed, my left "foot" jolted up—feeling electrically shocked every three or four minutes—in pain. My mind had informed my foot that a jumper cable had been attached to my two tiny toes. Then, an electric arc sparked from the live, attached car battery, which assaulted my entire missing appendage. This occurrence happened over and over consistently throughout my slumber. It jarred me awake each time.

But, the **most grueling** phantom pain, which I concluded as the highest, most excruciating *(levels 9 to 10+)*, felt like someone shot my fingers off with a revolver, instantly without warning. *BANG! BANG!* Or much like a nail or a spike had been driven into my "previous" palms. *CLANG! CLANG! CLANG!*

~*~

One day I woke up from this debilitatingly severe shooting pain. An instant lightbulb went off in my mind—*How was Jesus Christ crucified? Jesus felt those spikes driven into His hands and nailed through His feet.*

I tried to wrap my mind around this fact. I was blown away by the realization, and I rejoiced right then and there. I had the immense privilege to encounter this exponential agony that most people could never fathom! I continued to share with others, "This phenomenon was such a blessing. I experienced and received just a *'fractional glimpse'* of how Jesus, The Christ, had died for me." Truly wonder-stricken moments for sure. What a privilege to be reminded often—through flooded tears of pain—of that intense agony Jesus endured for me, for the world. I am still amazed as I process that idea logically, knowing what a sacrificial payment He made for all my sins.

By the grace of God, I rarely receive these excruciating levels of pain much now. Spikes, nails, or bullets are seldom driven or shot through my feet, palms, or fingers. He has often delivered me from this stark, realistic pain. But when I experience these painful reminders, I recollect once again the *payment* that Jesus paid on my behalf. His sacrifice proves how incredible and never-ending His love is for me.

~*~

A year after surgery, I began to contemplate how and when I could get off my medications for physical pain and phantom pain. I was nervous about doing so at first. My pain management physician *(Remember Dr. Warm N. Kind-Hearted?)* told me that it is uncommon to become an addict in an older age group. It is quite a bit easier to become hooked if younger. This kind and compassionate doctor knew I did not possess an addictive personality. Plus, I received a much lower dose than most to begin my regimen. It only had increased once while I worked with my new prosthetic legs or to achieve pain-free sleep.

After 18 months, I had slowly weaned off all my physical pain meds. And currently, I am taking only ONE phantom non-narcotic nerve blocker pill per day to ensure a restful night's sleep. I currently have been taken down in its potency as well. I am thrilled with this plan. I wouldn't say I like ingesting ANY medications that I don't feel are needed. I now relate to those who suffer from daily, devastating, debilitating pain. I don't take their prayer requests lightly anymore.

~*~

I am not the only one who endures horrific pain. I am in good company. As humans, we all experience misery in different ways, at different levels, in different often seasons of life. Pain is a certainty at some point in one's existence. During this COVID-19 pandemic, many are isolated. Numerous loved ones were forced to die in hospitals alone. Others have suffered from physical difficulties or emotional scars. There are now much too frequent statistics of high suicides and drug overdoses. Financial pains of lost incomes, financial hardships, or businesses forced to close. Also, relational issues of abuse, addictions, oppressions, even hunger are evident. And now, deep depressions from a divided country and COVID worries still exist.

America's economy shut down at one point. Pains were manifested layer upon layer. State governments not only closed our churches but also locked down our sporting events. Not only schools were emptied, but restaurants, too. All beauty appointments, beach vacations, and bridal/baby showers were canceled. Traveling had initially been affected all across the transportation industry. Families could no longer unite in large groups for holidays, celebrations, birthdays, graduations, births, weddings, anniversaries, vacations, and even funerals.

Social media has helped. We virtually stayed connected a bit, but it doesn't come close to that longed-for, physical connection. Humans need hugs, kisses, dating rituals, pats on the back, singing and praying together, crying, laughing, camping, corporate worshipping, etc. Such expansively horrible lists of setbacks and pitfalls.

America's 244th birth of Independence on July 4th this year was not celebrated in a typical manner due to the COVID-19 virus. Local community fireworks displays were canceled. *Highly unusual.* In all my sixty years, this cancellation of city fireworks shows had never occurred. Due to virus outbreaks and the resurgence of numbers, my birthday was not celebrated with sparklers in lieu of candles on my cake as in years past. No large gatherings of family and friends. Beaches were closed.

I became extremely disappointed. I had already missed the spectacular illumination bursts—due to illness—for the previous two years. I wonder how Mike and I are to share with our grandchildren and great-grandchildren our experiences, not only of my limb loss but also this worldwide 2020 pandemic?

As I looked back, my 2019 birthday was a do-over. Our family and close friends celebrated my 60th redo with the big Mission Viejo party. I had missed out the year before during my hospital shut-in. That day was extra special because I had survived the septic shock illness. I was very grateful to God for His healing. My faith in Him and the prayers of many allowed me to persevere and push through pain and adversity. Family members' love and care had also fueled my journey.

This year's birthday marked the second anniversary of the start of my unique health race. Some adverse complications and unfortunate roadblocks had begun two summers ago. But, don't forget, many spirit-led advantages amidst treasures of benefits were found along this open road, too. My *Life's* pink peg—placed next to my divine Father—kept me truckin' along without a worry, fear, or fret. God indeed became 'my hands and feet.'

I keep as much of a positive attitude as possible, no matter how much pain I must endure. Who wants to be around a grouchy old sourpuss anyway? *Not me!* God has met me daily in my pain. Jesus knew. He, too, had felt all my struggles. He gathered every tear I shed. I am confident in His continuing steadfast love and tenderness. I appreciate His kindness and patience as He strengthens my faith in Him each day. The wise God unfolds and reveals His ways slowly to me as I race through this path of pain. Since He is my ultimate chauffeur and companion, I can rest entirely in the backseat and let my Father lead the way.

I am dancing on my "Daddy's feet." He is leading me around life's dance floor.

~*~

I also experienced my second amputation anniversary on September 1st. I desired to move forward, not in reverse. I continued to invest wisely and consistently in God's guaranteed, treasured, heavenly crowns and rewards. As Apostle Paul encouraged Timothy, I also want to live in such a way as to hear these future words someday:

"His master said to him, 'Well done, good and faithful servant. You have been faithful over a little; I will set you over much. Enter into the joy of your master.'" Matthew 25:21

Amen. I can't wait.

Daily reading The Bible along with bravery, courage, and determination produced fuel through adversity. It became the horsepower I needed for quick bursts of speed and energy through pain and frustration. I still seek His power. I can't make this life journey alone. Gentleness, kindness, endurance, all linked with perseverance, are essential for the long haul. I rest in His abiding presence through prayers and thankfulness.

I want to end this chapter of *PUSHING THROUGH PAIN* with the words of the Apostle Paul in his pain...

"Three times I pleaded with the Lord about this *[thorn in his flesh]*, that it should leave me. But he said to me, 'My grace is sufficient for you, for My power is made perfect in weakness.' Therefore I will boast all the more gladly of my weaknesses, so that the power of Christ may rest upon me. For the sake of Christ, then, I am content with weaknesses, insults, hardships, persecutions, and calamities. For when I am weak, then I am strong." 2 Corinthians 12:8-10

God promised to be my strength in times of adversary. He holds me even without hands and feet—and all the pain associated with the loss of them—in His mighty grasp. I know that He will never let me go. The race is long and arduous. But God controls my pain and suffering. He's got this!

God has navigated my prosthetic journey as well. Pain will need to be revealed further in Chapter 6 when prosthetics crossed paths with pain. Take a spin with me in the next chapter—back to the wound unit—and verify how God ultimately sent others my way for my future body mechanics, mobility, and maneuverability.

BUT GOD...

"But the LORD has become my stronghold, and my God the rock of my refuge." Psalm 94:22

"My flesh and my heart may fail, but God is the strength of my heart and my portion forever." Psalm 73:26

"Be strong and courageous. Do not fear or be in dread of them, for it is the LORD your God who goes with you. He will not leave you or forsake you." Deuteronomy 31:6

CHAPTER 6

PROSTHETICS: PAIN, PITFALLS, and PLEASURES

"They have hands, but do not feel; feet, but do not walk; and they do not make a sound in their throat." Psalm 115:7

My first meeting with my extremely talented prosthetist, Rick Myers—*'Tricky Ricky'*—was in the Wound Care Unit of Long Beach Memorial Hospital a day or so after amputations. We were given his name and number from one of our pastors at Compass Bible Church who, it seemed, knew everyone.

Even though Mike did not phone him, Rick called us. He asked if he could visit to introduce himself. Recognizing his name, Mike apprehensively agreed. My sweet husband was overly cautious with me when I saw or interacted with visitors. I was so vulnerable, still sick with an infection. Rick came to only pray for me, pray for Mike.

This meeting was truly a pleasure. Rick did not even want to discuss the next steps of prosthetics. He was both friendly and caring. Mike and I knew right from that first visit, and as we moved forward, we chose to work with Rick and his Southern California Prosthetics team. During this next phase of my extremely hazardous course ahead, our newfound friend was willing and able to go to work for us. He began quickly and efficiently replacing my four flat tires.

Exceptional new tires for my damaged arms and legs were speedily ordered and manufactured through Rick and his team. These high-performance, top of the line, mag wheels would also need to be balanced. My racer's overhaul included a new timing belt, pistons, lube, gasket, and fuel from

Rick. Much like a Mobil Service Station, we chose this highly competent mechanic who owns and runs the prosthetic company SCP. We found that Rick and his wife lived a mile from our home. His shop was roughly ten minutes away. Many of his clients came from hundreds of miles, and some even traveled from many states away. We were very blessed. Rick developed and managed all these essential needed products and services for me. We designated Rick as our CEO for the job. Not only for his expertise in prosthetic excellence but also his compassion and love for his Lord.

Pit stop, but not a pitfall yet.

A few days after our meeting, Rick returned to Long Beach. He brought with him some shrinkers for my arm stumps and another set for my legs. Shrinkers are like tight, cotton compression socks put on over amputated limbs so that the skin begins to shrink post-surgery.

The goal was to dwindle my limbs' edema—all four ends—to a more cone-like shape. Shrinkage became the main objective for a much easier fit for prosthetics. When Rick came back a third time at the end of that week, he made a cast of both my legs right there in my hospital bed. The surgeon had already removed the staples. He made silicone liners and leg sockets from those molds.

As I mentioned before, my leg surgeon wanted me up and walking early within a three-four week timespan. Therefore, Rick had made that happen sooner than he thought my scars, strength, and pain level would have been ready. He also needed to comply with the doctor's orders. "*Yessir*," with a smile and salute. Vaguely, he only hinted to me then that it was too early to begin this painful process. My arduous road of early prosthetics was both extremely agonizing and perilous.

"He [God] gives power to the faint, and to him who has no might he increases strength. Even youths shall faint and be weary, and young men shall fall exhausted; but they who wait for the LORD shall renew their

146

strength; they shall mount up with wings like eagles; they shall run and not be weary; they shall walk and not faint." Isaiah 40:29-31

~*~

After amputations, I stayed three and a half weeks upstairs with my wound warriors—my critical care buddies. I was not allowed to transfer from the wound unit to the rehab center on the first floor unless I could endure their grueling schedule—two hours of physical therapy and one hour of occupational therapy every day but Sunday. I convinced them that I was up for the challenge, even though I knew that I was either bluffing or highly optimistic. So, I was allowed to enter the final lap of my recovery.

Rehabilitation Floor, here I come!

A few days after I had arrived in rehab, Rick had made prior arrangements for two of Long Beach Rehab's physical therapists to assist him with my first steps. Mike, a few family members, plus my wheelchair, and I met Rick down the hall to the workout room at the Long Beach Memorial Rehabilitation Center. Remember, I was only about 21 days post amputations. A physical therapist hooked a gait (*timing*) belt around my waist for safety. Rick asked gingerly, "Are you ready for this?" My son-in-law was patiently eager to capture the prosthetic setup and my first step on video. *Smile.*

Rick showed me my new "wheels." He lubed my legs all up with a greasy product before he put on the silicone liners. Liners were sprayed inside with rubbing alcohol mixed with water and rolled bottom-up my leg tightly—no air bubbles. Layers of cotton socks came next. Finally, black-sleeved leg sockets with shoes were fashioned on last. Tiffani already had brought Rick my tennis shoes that had been laced onto these counterfeit feet. They were ready to walk once again.

But was I?

Just getting my actual remaining legs lubed was painfully tender. I grimaced a bit and quickly realized that I was not even up on them yet. *Yikes!* After I had practiced several launches out of the wheelchair, I finally stood up fully—then froze. I hung on to Rick's shoulders without hands as he sat in a rolling chair in front of me. I apprehensively took my first and only step on my newly-fitted wheels. My eyes must have registered the intense pain because Rick had me sit right back down into the wheelchair behind me.

"Well, that's what your surgeon asked me to do. Now you will be on *my* schedule." Rick was gentle and thoughtful towards me every step through my custom prosthetic timetable. I knew then that I could trust him since he had my back—*or should I say legs!* Rick left with my new mobile customized back tires that day. My actual physical legs needed much more conditioning, and he knew I was not quite ready.

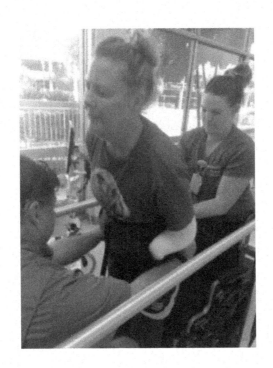

Pain-Induced First Steps

I cannot recall just how many rooms and hospital beds I had been convalescing in during these months—way too many, for sure. I had to move rooms only twice in Long Beach. The first reason was that they, too, were experiencing their own overhaul—a remodel. I moved from a beautiful spacious room with a pullout bed for Mike or Tiffani to a 'tool closet' they barely could call a room. That was okay. I didn't complain...much.

The second move was after I contracted C.DIFF *(Clostridium Difficile Bacterium or C. Difficile Infection)*. This additional illness was an intestinal bug that required three consecutive treatments of antibiotics. This infection sometimes occurs in hospital environments. For me, it began in my gut. I contracted this intestinal bug because of all of the numerous antibiotics I took for my survival. Antibiotics can destroy your good bacteria needed for healthy digestion. Some symptoms were nausea, fatigue, gut pains, cramping, dehydration, and diarrhea. My clean-ups were every hour throughout several days. *Thank you, CNAs and nurses, for your help and care!*

How do hospital physicians combat C-DIFF? MORE Antibiotics!

The first antibiotic was wimpy. My Infectious Disease Doctor—'*Where D. Go*'—had stopped by and visited with me every day at Long Beach Memorial. But, only at the beginning. When the first antibiotic was unsuccessful, he prescribed a second alternative. There were only three available that may cure the problem. But, after a couple of days into its ten-day regimen, I informed him that the hearing in my right ear was affected. My equilibrium was off. Dizziness became apparent. A type of vertigo had begun. The massive hearing loss happened rapidly. This struggle became a pitfall, indeed. He took me off this medication, but I never saw him again after revealing my acute hearing loss.

I lost total and permanent hearing in my right ear either from my extreme severe sepsis damage or from the *known* side-effect of this second antibiotic. I must have received enough to fight the gut infection because my symptoms diminished.

~*~

The first week of PT and OT workouts was brutal. When these demanding five days of reclamation rehab had just about passed, a major temporary foul-up was discovered at my expense. After I had completed my Friday's PT morning of a two-hour workout, I began to experience severe chills and nausea. *Why is this happening?* I begged off on my OT hour still scheduled for later that afternoon.

I relayed to Mike an hour or so later of my misery. "If I didn't know any better, I would think that I am having a withdrawal attack." I didn't comprehend what that truly felt like, but I had witnessed enough junkies on television who tried to kick their habits without a gradual decrease.

Unbeknownst to me or Mike, the rehab director—'*Director Doctor Discomfort*' *(Triple D)*—had taken me off my phantom pain meds cold-turkey! The day after I arrived and got settled into rehab, he conducted an intake evaluation. He asked me if I had experienced any phantom pain yet. I told him that I had not.

(For clarification, my surgeon upstairs had prescribed a dose of 300 milligrams 3 times a day for a substance that relieved this type of pain. I had no idea. Apparently, my leg surgeon had kept me on this dose. So, I still was on this regimen after transfer.)

This new director had not slowed me gradually down off of it. He had sideswiped me directly into an open pit. *Director DD* took me off *all* 900mg instantly that day, hence my severe symptoms. That circumstance felt to me as if I had raced the previous lap with a full tank of gas and had adequately powered my racer going into the final distance. When suddenly, I veered out-of-bounds into a wide-open trench. My fuel thoroughly drained

151

out because some cement block caused a hole in my gas tank. The following words were how I perceived my backsliding situation:

No fuel...meant no power...which meant no win.

Mike confronted the rehab director with the simple knowledge he found on the Internet. It was apparent even to a patient's husband that he should have gradually weaned me off. Mike was pretty furious when he learned of the screw-up. My husband told him that he expected an apology to me for that obvious blunder. With no apology offered from *DDD*, Mike mentioned his pharmaceutical error during my next early morning round-table discussion. Two Director Trainee Physicians appeared quite shocked at this revelation but wisely did not comment. Their mentor was found to be careless and irresponsible.

This pitfall, luckily for me, was brief. I fired back up and refueled through prayers again. I joined my PT and OT trainers the following morning for my 3-hour workout. They all worked me to the core for my core. Life again had rocked my little world, yet God had refilled my tank to overflowing once more.

I had been in the rehab center for two weeks total. The director wanted me to stay an additional week, but I ached to get out of there sooner rather than later. It had already been far too long being shuffled from one hospital to the next. I yearned to hit the road again and head home to my family. At the time, our only beloved grandchild, Jet William, was to celebrate his first birthday that weekend in our town. I longed to be home to watch him open his gifts with the rest of my clan.

So, when the rehab director came into my private room, he informed me that I had done well so far. But, he felt I needed one more additional week to practice basic movements and transfers. I had learned how to slide from my bed into a chair, wheelchair, or a car and back again. I had been taught several exercises on strengthening my core muscles to turn over from a prone position. I had been strongly encouraged to use my elbows for leverage. He knew, rightly so, I still required the third week to complete their schedule and improve many more exercises. All were needed for my strength and mobility before I should head home.

I looked at *DDDirector* and plainly spoke as if I had any authority, "No, that's not possible. I am going home tomorrow."

He looked at me with an authoritatively questioning look of his own which implied that I wasn't going anywhere. At least not yet. He probed further, "Why do you think you're going home tomorrow?"

And I flatly told him, "I'm going home tomorrow due to the fact I'm not missing my only grandbaby's first birthday celebration!"

But he asked me, "How are you going to do that if I don't release you?"

I looked him squarely in the face and replied, "Because my family will bust me out of here if you don't!"

With a shocked look on his face, he quietly admitted defeat. "Well then, OK."

That was the end of that discussion. *Doc DD* proceeded to tell the nurse— *who was chuckling under her breath*—to get the paperwork started. I was going home tomorrow. *Yay!* The simple pleasures of home. I couldn't wait to get back on the road again. This journey was taking far too long for my liking. Get me home, please. I gladly designated this turnpike stretch *"HOMEWARD BOUND."* I was heading home, and this 'vehicle' was raring to GO!

The following day around 10 am, Mike strolled into my room, and I felt like a little kid excited to go to Disneyland for the first time. He gathered up my personal items, which remained. My incredible spouse walked these gifts from friends and family—toiletries, pictures, flowers, food—out to the car to bring home with us. He pulled his car around to the side door of the rehabilitation workout room. I was so thrilled to be headed home after three long, l-e-n-g-t-h-y months of being in four different hospitals—five if you count rehab. I was so thankful to God for this milestone, which I thought would never come.

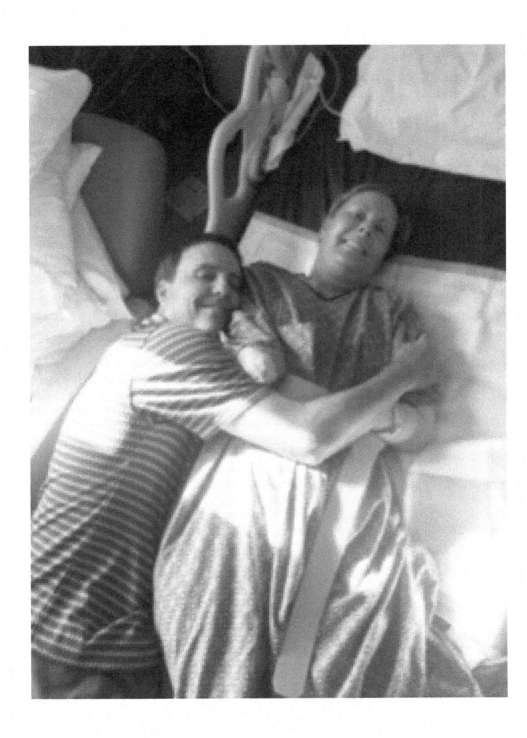

Earlier that morning, my C.DIFF woes returned. I was a bit worried. *Was I still infected?* Staff informed me, as my stomach churned and bowels cramped, that this was normal due to the excitement and nerves of the next phase towards home. I wanted to believe them because those in authority would have re-admitted me upstairs again. Back to the start. More tests. More cultures. MORE antibiotics.

So, I dropped my concerns. I desired to be home.

There always is a ton of paperwork when one checks into a hospital, but especially so when leaving. The rehabilitation center director, the hospital administration personnel, the disabilities advocate, two CNAs, my morning and afternoon nurses, and my physical and occupational therapists were all there with me in my last hospital room. They said their goodbyes. Mike began to sign the final stack of paperwork as my CNA headed me out to be wheeled down the corridor for the last time. I felt free. I felt thankful. I felt blessed to be alive! My unbelievably most difficult, pain-filled work of ongoing rehab and prosthetics had barely just begun. But, at least I would be back home within the hour.

As my CNA pushed the disability button to open the automated door, the checkered flag was poised to wave. Although I struggled over the final feet of the walkway, I had, indeed, crossed this finish line. Liberating! It opened before me the autumn sun's warmth and assurance. Mike had just pulled his car around and faced the passenger door towards my wheelchair with a smile of joy and apprehension. Slide-board out and new timing belt on, we found out I *was* capable and strong enough to transfer into an actual vehicle. But not with much finesse or sophistication. Satisfaction guaranteed.

Victory lap...

I had not ridden in a car since the night Mike had driven me back with Tiff and Mike W to my first hospital in Placerville. What a strange feeling as we drove at high freeway speeds. *Exhilarating!* I headed home excited for a party. We traveled roughly the same distance of 42 miles from Long Beach to home as we had traveled originally from the Sierra Mountains to Placerville. Ninety-two days had passed between these two races. *Dreamlike.* In my mind, it had felt like an eternity.

~*~

Many people were there waiting for me as Mike pulled his Toyota Camry into our driveway. A much-enjoyed pleasure, for sure. Balloons. Decorations. A new ramp for my wheelchair. My transfer gait belt and slide board got me safely out of the car. More flowers, plants, and fun fall decor from two Home Fellowship Group ladies brought smiles.

But the most extraordinary delight was when I saw my family as they stood outside in our front yard. They clapped and clapped. Most cried with tears of joy, and I was thrilled beyond words. My hospital journey thus far had come to a close. My 'car' had returned to its rightful winner's spot after it had crossed the finish line in First Place. With God driving, we had won the race. Everyone present knew how much this moment meant to me to be home. Finally home!

We hugged. We kissed. We cried. I remember that day like it was yesterday. My siblings and their spouses, my children and their spouses, my dad, and our one-year-old-to-be grandson had greeted me like I was a queen—their *'Homecoming Queen.'* Such a perfect, yet meaningful, homecoming.

The party for Jet and of my return home was satisfactorily celebrated the next day. I don't believe that Baby Jet knew what was happening, but that didn't seem to matter. What mattered most and brought happiness to all was that friends and family celebrated together. Guess who showed up? Rick Myers. Before the party began, when preparations were being finalized, he wheeled me to our beautiful Mission Viejo fall-struck backyard. He wanted to take updated, second castings of my legs.

Now that demonstrated *Tricky Ricky's* dedication to me.

After all family members had been introduced to my new prosthetist, he got straight to work and cast both legs once again. Because I wore those shrinkers religiously for those last couple of weeks at rehab, brand new sockets needed to be remade as well as the silicone liners. What commitment to his craft and his patients. Rick quickly made his casts and hurried out after he had prayed with me once again. We both thanked God that I was home, healthy, and ready for the prosthetic legs. He manufactured the next set within days that following week.

But, I was *not* healthy. My hunch, the day I was discharged, was correct. C.DIFF had returned. What a burden for my loved ones. I needed the third and only antibiotic left in their toolbox. *And The Most Costly!* One dosage costs $5,000 for ten pills. I told Mike he had better drive an armored truck to pick them up at our local pharmacy. Our Blue Shield Case Manager *'Miss Marvelous'* had gone to great lengths for us and gained approval from their specialist board of physicians.

If this highly-priced medication had not eradicated this complicated bacterial infection, I would have required additional surgery for the implantation of healthy fecal cultures. AND more antibiotics. I prayed, *'Please God, I need Your healing hands yet again.'*

I thanked God for providing for us financially through my teachers' insurance policy Blue Shield of California. Our bank account would not be adversely affected by this fiery trial. We were gratefully delighted. Insurance paid out millions of dollars for all my surgeries, ICU occupancy, tests, medications, surgeons' and physicians' fees, hospital stays, staff care, equipment, prosthetics, and exponentially more.

~*~

Rick even made house calls. I was extremely nervous when he called and relayed to Mike or Tiff that he was coming over. This faithful prosthetic servant showed up for either a fitting or for me to test drive the new legs a week or so later. Sometimes selfishly, I prayed that he would not call. The pain was still a significant factor—a bonafide pitfall towards recovery. But inevitably, he showed up with devotion and compassion in his eyes. Rick looked upon me as his sister. Honestly, he is my brother in Christ.

It frightened me to think as I continued to heal that I needed to place my tender legs, which were still quite raw, into a hard, constricted socket. It was an early requirement that I attempted to use them as stilts to stand up and balance. But then walk, too? Remember, I was fragile, and it took all my strength, energy, and pain medication to endure what Rick asked me to do. He was the expert, and I was not. He was the prosthetist, and I was his patient. He was a brother who cared, and I was his petrified sister who put on a brave face everyone with which I came in contact. A definite drawback was pain.

This suffering was scary stuff. I had never felt so frightened, but at the same time, I realized I needed to succeed. What would my life look like if I never walked again? That terrified me. I understood that my family, especially Mike and Tiffani, would have to transfer and push me around everywhere in my wheelchair—an extra *50 pounds*—for the rest of my life. Was I to be forever sidelined? No way. That was not an option. I worked diligently, of course, which was the agonizingly proper thing to do no matter how much strength and endurance it took. It was both hazardous (falls) and difficult (lack of strength and super painful).

Rick showed Mike, Tiffani, and my sister-in-law Brenda how to fasten on my legs. Even now, it is a distinct process. The first layer that goes on my skin is a petroleum jelly-like product. Early on, it extremely hurt because it was slathered all over my amputated leg area. Rick told my family members when I first got home, "Gently, gingerly massage the ends of Vicki's legs often." The pain was barely tolerable. After they pursued this task for many days, several times a day, and my legs began to heal more and more, the pain lessened.

My wonderful prosthetist was also an excellent resource for much more than just artificial limbs. SCP staff worked in conjunction with a pain management physician whose place of business also provided in-house rehabilitation. *'Dr. Warm N. Kind-Hearted'* was THE BEST physician that took me under his wing when I got home. His caring compassion for all of us—Mike, Tiffani, Mike W, and me—was priceless. He made sure to manage me as a whole, complete patient. He was not just all about pain. He cared for me as a medical expert, cherished friend, and treasured brother.

Rick sent me to this man soon after I arrived home that early October. This same *Dr. WNK (Wink)* prescribed meds for both physical pain and phantom pain. He understood when I was too frightened to ween off my pharmaceuticals. But, gradually, this considerate doctor had done just that. By a year and a half after my life-threatening episode, he had me off all narcotics. Slowly, calmly, deliberately each month, he gave me the confidence I needed to trust his expertise. He calmed my apprehension. He became my pain and pill liberator.

We discussed not only my pain and therapeutics, but he included ideas surrounding my prosthetics. We discussed "how to" tricks, tools, and tasks, which assisted me in understanding my new normal better. For the most beneficial operation of these artificial marvels, this beloved physician, Tiffani, Alistair, and Rick, taught me their exceptional first-rate uses. All four were like a team of NASCAR *(National Association for Stock Car Auto Racing)* mechanics that worked on the entire race-car for optimum performance and reliability. This competitive motorist appreciated all their efforts on my behalf.

Doctor Kind-Hearted shared his plan, perception, and viewpoint of what my life should look like as I moved forward as a quadrilateral amputee. My mobility, dexterity, flexibility, maneuverability, along with my frame of mind, pain tolerance, and sleep, were paramount in his mind and mine. I wanted to become the best I could be, not only for me but for the rest of my family and others.

This amazing pain/rehab professional wanted the best for me as well. *Thanks, Doc!* I have referred a handful of friends and family members with their own set of pain problems to *Dr. Wink,* with confidence.

~*~

Even though mentioned previously, here is the entire leg process from start to finish each day:

First, a layer of petroleum jelly (lube) is slathered on each end of both legs. After the petroleum jelly layer is applied, the silicon liners need to be put on next. This process requires 50% alcohol-50%water (fuel) sprayed into the liner and rolled backward up my leg, making sure that the left slides over my left leg and the right slides onto my right leg. Highly customized, much like some of my former car covers.

They cannot be put on backward either—notches touch my shin bone in the front. These liners are roughly fourteen inches long. A perfect fit, but over time a new pair was needed to be swapped out as my legs began to shrink even more. I recently had a small rip in my right liner directly on the back of my kneecap. Its seal was broken; air escaped. This (air-filter) needed replacement. So, I switched to my alternate pair.

The subsequent layers are cotton socks that do not look like regular socks that someone else would put on their feet. These multi-layers of socks resemble more like something one would wear over a swollen knee cap. Their size—*at least for me*—was approximately 4" x 8" tubular shape with one end closed. (Like cotton, stretchy pillowcases). Luckily, I only needed to don these to minimize pain for six months.

161

Layer four consists of one sheath *(nylon sock)* that pulls up to about an inch below each silicone liner. These sheaths resemble knee-high nylons that I had worn previously with slacks and heels to work or church.

And last, the prosthetic legs get put on fairly snug with a thick, black sleeve attached to each socket. These rubber inside and stretchy-cloth outside sleeves get rolled up backward to a mid-thigh level covering the silicone liners.

This entire apparatus made for a vacuum-sealed leg that cannot be pulled off or would not fall off on its own. I know when air is escaping from each tiny hose in the back of the socket because I either hear escaping air with each step—*rather embarrassing!*—or I feel it bubbling as the liner has escaping air inside during each step that I take. Now, after two years, Mike can get my legs—*wheels*—on in approximately five minutes. My invaluable NASCAR pit worker.

This appendage has a flesh-colored foot on which I can put any shoe. I was pleased to find out that I wore the exact same shoe size 6-1/2 as I had before. I may also change shoes anytime or with each season. The feet stay anchored. My ankles consist of metal rods about two inches in diameter. The metal is then attached with a 4-screw plate to the socket, which my stump resides. My leg's calf muscle is just a little off the bottom of the socket.

Currently, I have a purple-toned—*my favorite color*—socket. I get to choose which pattern, style, or color with each socket-pair made. The duo I am currently wearing is my 3rd set so far. Attached to the sockets are the black sleeves that roll up each amputated leg. It looks very high-tech to me.

My ankle does not bend, and since it is stationary, I need to walk what I call the "snowman walk." Lift up, down, lift up, down—*much like pistons.* I am currently walking with a normal gait, so it doesn't look like I am marching but striding. My fake ankles do not inflect; therefore, I cannot point or flex these toes. Presently, I am attempting to get myoelectric feet—*approved and paid by insurance*—where the ankle is hinged. I will then go up and down hills, inclines, and steps much more effortlessly.

During one of my sessions with my new legs, Subtle Rick was no longer behind me, making sure I did not fall. This particular time, my sister-in-law Brenda accompanied me, and she realized she should walk directly behind me for safety reasons. All of a sudden, Rick Costco bumped her gently out of the way on purpose. She got his hint that I was to do this lap around SCP's room on my own. I spied this happening through my peripheral vision, and Brenda looked at me as if to say, *'Sorry Vic, I can't be there to help you. So, whatever you do, don't fall on my watch.'*

The following week, the next feat with my new feet was to venture outside on the paved walkway around Rick's SCP prosthetic rehab center. Rick also wanted to witness my stamina to see how far I could walk on my own. One of his assistants walked behind me with a wheelchair while Rick walked right next to me as we talked. Of course, I had on my safety gait belt. Rick was convinced I could walk about 100 yards to the end of the complex and back. I made it to the end, sat down in the wheelchair for a few minutes, and then resumed my walk and made it another 60 yards back.

Yay! This stroll was another victorious milestone to be celebrated for sure—Frapy's chocolate yogurt on the way home.

I chose tennis shoes for my first year on my artificial feet—'my training wheels'—for stability. This summer, I sported a more natural look—barefoot with sandals. Mike even painted my fake, realistic toenails bright pink, as I had before. He draws the line, though, with not adding flower designs! Soon, this upcoming fall/winter season, I want to change to zip-up boots. *Fashionable*. Realize one thing; I'm not trying to hide my skinny ankles. They're my fashion statement.

I have walked on my prosthetic legs without a wheelchair now since Christmas Eve, 2018. I praise the Lord that this is so. For explanation, I began with one hour daily, then worked up and added an additional hour each week. I have only fallen one time. I stepped down a step in our master bedroom and spun to protect my artificial left arm and hand. So, the brunt of my fall was shock-absorbed on the muscle tissue of my upper arm. That could have caused a major injury and setback. But, Rick instructed me how to fall correctly. He told me several times, "The worst thing a leg amputee could do would be to fall backward!" I don't think of my legs much once they are on—such a blessing. I keep them on all day until Mike takes them off at bedtime.

It wasn't easy to walk with balance when I had not much remaining arm left. I waited a bit for shrinkage and swelling to go down from my residual limbs because a tight fit is essential for artificial arm, hand, and finger mobility. Arms are complicated to cast, manufacture correctly, and electrodes adequately placed. They are much more technical than legs.

I kept hearing about an arms expert who lives in Florida who works with Rick and his Florida partner Stan. I even sent Alistair a video taken of me as I walked around SCP with my new prosthetic legs. And my amputated arms with their shrinkers on were exposed. Even though I had never met Alistair on this part of the track, I begged him to come quickly. Rick flew Alistair— my *'Scottish-Buddy'*—to California as an expert arm prosthetist just for me.

Six months after amputations, Alistair flew out and took casts of my arms. It was a delightful pleasure to meet Alistair finally. We had heard so many positive things about him. He utilized a company here on the West Coast to manufacture the sockets, so the turnaround time was only two days. *Thanks, Frank!* Alistair also came to train Tiffani (OT) and other members of Rick's prosthetic staff. Rick's recently hired team members needed to acquire knowledge and CE credits regarding upper extremities. I did not mind being a test-driver for this awesome NASCAR Team. Alistair became my *"go-to"* guy for my arm prosthetics' initial success.

Alistair had to locate my muscles in the top and bottom of each forearm. That way that the electrodes inside the sockets would trigger the opening and closing of each bionic hand. Muscles I still possess today. Since my first two arm sockets were manufactured in 2019, Rick and Alistair, along with Frank, Macky D, YV, Tee Cee, Ash *(as I nicknamed them),* Tiff, now others, are fully qualified to repair these technological breakthroughs. As I claimed, God put together this fantastic squad to assist me in my mobility and dexterity needs.

So by that particular Sunday morning, I was properly fit with my new arms. *Terribly exciting!* Arm sockets were manufactured flesh-colored, and Alistair and Frank left a gap cutout for my elbow to bend and straighten. These new arms have an on/off switch which I love if they start to go rogue. They sometimes develop a mind of their own, especially in the mornings. I tell Mike a couple of times a week, "Okay, my hands are being naughty today," until they get warmed up.

Each synthetic arm also has an air valve to push and release the air for a tighter fit, just like tires. Under the switch is a small circular silver battery charger. Mike plugs these electricity-required sockets complete with detachable hands into a power source. Since I wear them all day and my legs, these arms must be charged every night, much like an electric car. This process—which I warned— resembled a vehicle in a Mobil Full-Service Station's garage area.

The first set of standard hands purchased was flesh-looking but only opened and closed in a pincher-type fashion. I was even excited to try these out with guidance from Alistair and Christy *(a woman who is an OT employee for the company OSSÜR, which sold us my new hands).* She trained Tiffani as I learned how to operate these new miracles. It was like I had learned a new video game. It was wonderful! I had not had hands for approximately seven months.

Whenever others see my robot hands—especially the young ones—I am almost always asked, "How do you make your hands work?" My response..."I bend my wrist I no longer have—*but I still have it in my mind.* I move my 'wrist' forward to close the hand. I move my 'wrist' back to open the hand." Very high-tech!

Muscles in my forearms trigger the movements. Try this experiment to understand better: Hold one forearm with the opposite hand. Now, wiggle your fingers. Do you feel forearm muscles moving? That is what my muscles do for me.

To make the hand spin around, I must co-contract both forearm muscles— *top and bottom*—simultaneously to activate the spin mode. On my right hand, that requires a quick clench of my *"imaginary"* fist. But on my left hand, I *"think"* about my human hand and flick out those original first two fingers quickly and wait until I hear a beep.

So to eat with my prosthetic left hand—*which is longer for stability,*

- I open my left hand (wrist back),

- put a fork facing down between my prothetic first two fingers,

- close my hand (wrist forward),

- flick out quickly my first two fingers (*in my mind*),

- listen for the beep.

- The fork, which is then stabilized, goes down.

- It picks up food and rotates it up to my mouth

- by moving my "wrist" *(forward and backward)*

- Which moves my fork up and down.

I no longer have authentic wrists that rotate. Remember, this is all done in my mind using wrists and fingers that I no longer have. I can even still count and move my fingers that I used to have. The sensations are still with me in my mind.

Crazy? Insane.

What was my first official lunch using my new arms? *Chick-fil-A.* I was able to learn the process above fairly quickly with relative success. But by the time I got it down perfectly with Tiff's assistance, encouragement, and motivation, my arms had shrunk inside the socket. I could no longer co-contract to make them work properly. This learning process was frustrating for Tiffani and me because we felt like I had it working so well. But within a week, the arms were no longer functional.

Back to the shop. Pitfall once again.

That entire training needed to be scrapped and started over. But this next time, I received what I dubbed my "super-charged" high-tech hands. I was able to put on my own make-up. I don't apply mascara, mind you, because it's too difficult to unscrew the cap.

Prosthetics are known as body parts, so a person cannot just sell them on eBay, Facebook Marketplace, or Craigslist. It's not one size fits all. They're custom-made just for me. Therefore, my arms must be refit, and my team of experts would start the entire process over each time my arms shrunk or changed. Two months later, I was recast again but religiously wore my shrinkers as much as possible before my appointment date. I wished not to go through this ordeal again any time soon.

With my newest arm sockets and hands working again, Tiffani had decided that she could have me fully trained in using these new arms and hands for whatever I needed to do on my own by the end of the summer. That's when we all moved out of our two-story home. Mike and Tiff moved out and began preparations for their baby boy, who was due in early November.

So Tiffani and I set out and made a list of all the jobs and tasks I wanted to accomplish on my own when she was no longer with me. Of course, I wanted to learn to eat, use the restroom alone, brush my hair and teeth, put on my make-up, put a load of laundry in the washing machine, turn on the dryer, open the refrigerator, etc. Every day we tackled one of these jobs. Tiff instructed me to ergonomically move my shoulder and use my new prosthetic hands to gain confidence and agility with each task.

"Whatever your hand finds to do, do it with your might..." Ecclesiastes 9:10

These new hands are not flesh look-a-likes. They resemble a robotic look— black individualized fingers with a mechanical yet manually movable thumb *(picture Terminator)*. Overtop for protection were black gloves that I switched out for opaque white. The black *'Terminator'* [1] fingers mixed with the white silicone gloves make them appear grayish. Mike and I didn't want to look daily at black hands. Those reminded us both of my black, mummy skin. We wished to leave that memory in the dust.

Many don't comprehend—*I had no clue*—that as an amputee who is missing fingers, I can still 'count' all my fingers in my mind. I move each of my 'fingers' as I count...1, 2, 3, 4, 5. My mind computes that I am moving them. My nerves which used to attach and flow through my fingers, now buzz ruthlessly and tingle fretfully with each finger that bends in my mind as I count them off one right after the other. The muscles in my forearms move during this process.

I can share precisely my current mind's position of my left-hand fingers. On your mark...get set...count!

Thumb positioned straight out. Pointer finger points up to ceiling nice and tall. Middle finger bent in half at its knuckle. Ring finger and pinky pressed together positioned down towards the floor. I am amazed at what the mind can do. Maybe someday, biomedical engineers will develop a hand that mimics the exact brain signals so each individualized finger could move independently. I would take pleasure in being the first quadrilateral amputee to experience this phenomenon.

What am I not able to do with my new hands? Well, it is almost impossible to pick up a tortilla chip, whereas they easily crumble and break. Other things that are most difficult: unscrew a cap of any type, turn and open round doorknobs, butter a piece of bread, or cut my food. I also cannot do dishes *(oh darn!)* or take my own shower because these hands cannot be submerged in liquids.

I pictured myself as The Bionic Women [2], with both legs and arms now fabricated, balanced, and calibrated to perfection. Oh, *sorry!*—The Bionic Nana. *'Robo-Nana'* to my family. *'Robo-Teacher'* during my STEAM lessons at my former elementary school.

~*~

That same mid-May, not even a year after amputations, and I found myself smack dab in sepsis protocol all over again! I felt just a little 'off' that morning when Tiffani asked me how I was feeling. She must have sensed that something was wrong. My chipper self was a little down, and I felt so tired. I told Tiffani at lunch that I was heading in a few hours with her dad for my scheduled 3 pm urology appointment. This incredible doctor always checked for urinary tract infections (UTI).

My urinalysis test was deemed positive, which determined that I did, in fact, have a UTI. Since the doctor knew my history, he told us that Mike would take me straight to the emergency room at Saddleback Memorial Hospital in our neighboring town if I began to run a fever. Mike dropped me off into my recliner at home. He left straight away for the pharmacy to fill my prescription for *another* antibiotic. Fifteen minutes later, I took the first dose. But by 4:30 pm, when an additional fifteen minutes had ensued, I experienced uncontrollable chills. I had precisely run a low-grade fever of 100.8°. Off we went to the ER.

Not again, Lord. HELP!

Soon after we arrived, checked in, and waited about 20 minutes, a nurse called me back. She had begun to draw blood for analysis. It was—*and still is*—extremely difficult to find my veins after amputations. The nurse brought Mike a bag for my belongings. My exorbitantly expensive prosthetic arms with hands were placed inside and held and guarded by Mike.

A charge nurse with much more experience was called to see if she could find a vein. I tried to be brave as she dug the needle deeper and rotated it around under my skin. She tried everything to locate that vein. I never looked, but I sure felt it. Since I had that first dose of the antibiotic, the nursing staff patiently waited anxiously to see what bacteria pulsed through my body this time. Right then and there, my instant thought:

I have been improving day by day. I do not want to backtrack. This is Déjà vu.

I experienced PTSD. I flashed back to my many prior surgeries that happened only nine months before.

Even though the urine and blood cultures were not conclusive yet, an admitting nurse brought me to an ER room with a bed while the cultures were still being analyzed. Mike took off my costly legs and added them to the bag he carried for my arms. These "parts" cost much, much more than any of our previously owned vehicles had cost. Tiffani, along with her husband Mike W, showed up after I was in my hospital gown. I wore their fuzzy hospital grip socks on my calves. All four of my shortened limbs were mega-exposed.

When they realized I was in good care, Tiff and Mike W wanted to know if I was hungry. By this time, the clock had ticked past dinner time. I was not allowed to eat because I may be having surgery that night. I told them to go somewhere to eat but to please bring Dad and me back something if I was allowed a meal. Within half an hour, it was verified that I was in the beginning stages of sepsis.

Again?

Sepsis protocols were immediately initiated. First, an ER doc prescribed a heavy-duty antibiotic. He administered this straight into my bloodstream through my intravenous tube, and fluids were added as well. This physician ordered a chest x-ray along with a CT scan. Sure enough, another kidney stone dropped once again out of my right kidney. *'Oh Lord, not this again,'* I prayed. I felt His peace once more while in this Southern California hospital's *fix-it garage*. Does the Lemon Law apply to me? I felt so sorry for Mike and the kids. Not again. I was so overwhelmed and confused by my new, but not yet improved, life. Many questions swirled in my mind.

What's happening, Lord? Show me Your Ways...

What do You want to teach me? Please open my heart to learn...

Why this setback now, God? Help me to rest in Your bigger plan...

Medical professionals determined that nothing additional would be done for me that night. Although, I was admitted into the hospital and prepped early in the morning for surgery by my very own expert urologist. I had just seen *'Dr. Hercules'* less than five hours before. Another stent was skillfully placed in my ureter to bypass this stone, too. He is one amazing surgeon. Only one problem, Saddleback Hospital's Infectious Disease Doctor administered an incompatible antibiotic. Upon hearing her prescription choice, I immediately informed her that this particular antibiotic had caused a rash early in my childhood. She verbalized and rationalized that it caused that rash numerous decades ago. She insisted and prescribed this particular med anyway. The antibiotic that was in my IV *did* cause an allergic reaction. *So Frustrating!* Of course, I had to stay an additional night post-surgery.

~*~

Mike and I planned to celebrate our 40th wedding anniversary that same weekend. We were not going to celebrate too far away. We were scheduled to leave the very next morning to make the trek back up to the cabin in Kyburz. That trip north would have marked the first time back since my entire ordeal had begun.

Unbelievable. Almost eleven months had passed. I figured we were medically forced to celebrate our milestone anniversary another time. We sadly stayed home as I recovered from surgery—another pitfall that caused just a few tears.

By the end of that month, when urologist *Dr. Hercules* removed the stent, he agreed that he should grab out all my kidney stones sooner rather than later. Three additional surgeries were performed within the following four months. Proactively, the 25 stones in each kidney were dealt with surgically. All the floaters were removed while this surgeon blasted the other smaller ones. Several remained lodged securely in the kidney wall, safe and sound, unable to drop.

Mike and I felt sidelined for a while. Once again, I became a travel invalid. We had absolute zero assurance that sepsis was way off in the distance, far from our raceway. It had attacked my body twice. When would it happen for the third time? A fourth? The infection had set me again into a spinning physical descent. Mike and I had concluded that I had once again turned into a spin. Was I ready to blow a gasket and drop a stone at every curve?

172

Remarkably, my doctor performed all of my kidney stone surgeries by October—exactly one year after I had arrived home from Long Beach Memorial's Physical Therapy Center, just as God had promised me the year before!

~*~

My prosthetic arms and legs are lifelines to my well-being and now are my new normal. They feel like my own after my post-amputation second anniversary. I used to ask my original fingers to complete countless detailed, dexterous, intricate jobs almost every second of every day. I never used to think about these former, supremely important digits. I praise God for the 60 years I had been given to use them.

I took my body parts for granted. No longer. My God takes care of me through my husband's loving deeds and prayers. I press onward through my new and challenging life. Just as Joni Eareckson Tada's closure before she signed off on her recent correspondences to me, *"Onward and upward."* Such encouragement she often delivers to me. Mike and I long to revisit Joni and Ken after California's lockdowns from this COVID-19 are over.

"Thank you, Friend Joni, for your valued friendship, perseverance through suffering, and your Godly example of a true Christ-follower."

As I advanced, Rick informed me that I would require new sockets for my arms and legs approximately every three years due to the body aging with future shrinkage. He also told me that *The National Amputee Association* wanted me to be their key-note speaker this year after the virus was under control around the country and when the U.S. was back open. I was told, out of 500,000+ amputee members, I utilize my prosthetic limbs with confidence, grace, and ease.

Rick told me recently, "Vicki. You are in the top 1% of amputee victims who use your upper extremities' prosthetics with great success. Most purchase them but quickly throw these marvels into a closet, never to be used again." This usage is not in my power but through God's marvelous work. My entire team is top-notch, and I am truly grateful.

Many amputees are extremely frustrated along their journey toward mobility. I assumed maybe that they chose to stay parked in their wheelchairs rather than up and mobile. Or I've heard from specialists that other amputees have decided they are too frustrated to continue to learn for proficiency. What a shame. Rather heartbreaking, actually. My advice: Don't stall out! Get back into the race. There is much more scenery to be enjoyed.

Here are words sent to Rick for his recent milestone birthday:

Dearest Rick,

Happy 60th Birthday!

Do you realize that Mike and I met you two years ago? I had my complicated quadruple amputations on September 1st, 2018. My second anniversary is today! But, in some ways, it feels like we have known you and your SCP Team for much, much longer...

You are my specialist in prosthetics.

You are my 'go-to' buddy in artificial limbs.

You are my mobility cheerleader.

You are my cherished friend.

You are my brother—my brother in Christ.

Words cannot do justice to my feelings of gratitude towards you. Mike and I value our friendship. May it ever grow stronger with each passing year. We owe you a birthday week at the cabin. But, we owe you exponentially more.

Happy Birthday, Dear Friend.

Love, Vicki

~*~

I mentioned before that I loved being a stay-at-home mom for David and Tiffani's early years. And, I have utterly thrived being married to a fabulous, God-honoring husband, Mike, for over four decades. He treats me, cares for me, and loves me so well. From the starting line of my near-death illness in early July of 2018 and on past the finish line of prosthetics and their learning curve, I have trusted my Lord and Savior. With each advancing mile of this challenging race, we overcame flames of heat through our faith. God has always been in control. Our intense testing refined to reveal in us our gold, silver, and precious stones.

Tested by Fire!

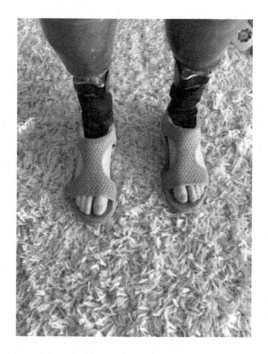

2nd Pair of Leg Sockets With Summer Sandals

"Now if anyone builds on the foundation with gold, silver, precious stones, wood, hay, straw—each one's work will become manifest, for the Day will disclose it, because it will be revealed by fire, and the fire will test what sort of work each one has done." 1 Corinthians 3:12-13

I scheduled this month to grab a quick oil change and slight tune-up at Rick's shop. I will also soon receive new arm sockets, a backup set, and updated waterproof hands. But, I won't be choosing my fresh legs' socket color for another two years or so. *Hmmm*, I'll be contemplating their next color. A lovely Easter-egg blue, perhaps?!?

"Onward and Upward" to greater heights in the next chapter on my route towards safety, serenity, and a secure future.

BUT GOD...

"But the Lord GOD helps me; therefore, I have not been disgraced; therefore I have set my face like a flint, and I know that I shall not be put to shame." Isaiah 50:7

"But I call to God, and the LORD will save me." Psalm 55:16

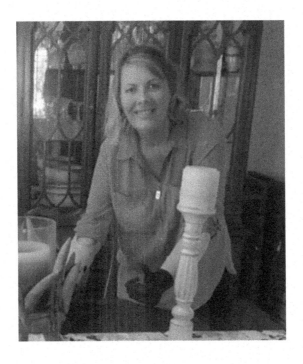

Dusting with Updated Arms

CHAPTER 7

PERFECT HOPE & PURE JOY

"May the God of hope fill you with all joy and peace in believing, so that by the power of the Holy Spirit you may abound in hope." Romans 15:13

Many people I meet inevitably ask me, "How do you stay so happy because I would absolutely fall apart if I lost even one hand or one foot!?!" All had tried to visualize themselves in my shoes. Even though I had been *'tested by fire,'* it was my strong faith in Jesus Christ that kept me focused and fueled. My roadster had moved me approximately 22,000 days—sixty years—closer towards the finish line.

But before I share another thought, I must make a U-turn and revisit the time when I totally surrendered my life to my Lord and Savior, Jesus Christ. It gives me great pleasure to cruise back to my *"spiritual"* starting line. Please join me as my road companion while I once again shift the car into reverse and journey back to an earlier time, an earlier place...

Faith Beginnings:

Mom and Dad (Bill & Carol Patterson) ensured that their four children were raised as churchgoers and hearing the Bible taught. They believed this was their Godly responsibility. All of us were dedicated to the Lord as infants. As we grew, both parents were unilateral in their approach as they strongly shaped our tender hearts toward Him. I knew I received the love of reading my Bible from my parents. They read biblical scriptures with me from my beautifully illustrated picture Bible when I was five.

My deep love for Jesus and His truth was discovered along the roadway as I traversed my spiritual journey. It ignited in me a deep faith in God from an impressionable age. This passion was due directly to Mom and Dad's perseverance.

I found many years ago the proper path towards an ongoing relationship with God. As a graduated fifth-grader, I realized what it meant to become "a Christian" during a summer Sunday morning worship service. I understood the true meaning of repentance and faith, especially the need to 'count the cost.'

I listened to a young missionary, *'Miss Congeniality'* from the African Congo, who was on furlough that year. She began to share her experiences with our congregation, who sponsored her financially. I listened intently, most likely because of her age (mid-20s), her passion for the people of Congo, and her most riveting slideshow.

The Holy Spirit spoke to my heart that morning. God impressed upon my soul that He wanted me to be a nurse in Africa when I grew up just as she was. I immediately, rebelliously, angrily, stubbornly thought, *'NO, GOD!'*

Within moments, I felt a strong, guilty twinge of disobedience in my gut.

I quickly turned to justification. *'I hate needles. I hate blood. By the way, LORD, I pass out when I even SEE blood. Not a missionary. Not a nurse. LORD! P-l-e-a-s-e!'* This command was not MY plan for MY life, even at this rookie age of eleven. Instantly, though, illumination of an opposing thought crossed my mind.

'Did I just now pray in my silent prayer, LORD? Is He truly Lord of my life, or am I lord of my own life? If I am fighting God and telling Him "NO" emphatically, then I am lord on the throne—not God.

Then came the begging. I BEGGED God not to send me to the Ivory Coast in West Africa. I had never even been on a plane, let alone flew to the other side of the world. I was so afraid. Scared, frightened, and petrified were words that came nowhere near what bubbled inside my heart, my mind, and my gut on that Sunday morning—The Lord's Day.

More closely PURE PANIC...an anxiety attack of a sort.

My heart pounded out of my chest. *(As I write this, I can still feel what it was like to firmly hold onto that unrelenting tension in my young, rebellious heart.)* I knew I wrestled with God—as Jacob wrestled God for a blessing in the Old Testament Bible story *[Genesis 32]* that my mother had read with me only a few short years before.

I continued to spar with God in my mind, heart, and soul for the entire eleven o'clock service. Finally, I recognized my rebellion and owned up to my sins of stubbornness, pride, arrogance, and short-sidedness. I was exhausted!

"OK God, I repent! You are in control. I trust you. I surrender. I'll do whatever you ask of me! YOU are on the throne!"

After I had repented (Jesus had already taken care of my sin problem on the cross), I removed my will and placed my total trust and confidence in Him. I finally put God on His rightful throne of my life. If The Almighty wanted me to go to the Ivory Coast, Congo, or Tanzania—across the entire breadth of Africa—I would go. This profound, debilitating fear and tension immediately dissipated.

God was pleased with my submission. I felt it in my heart. I knew it in my mind, and I found it to be true in my soul.

I understood—50 years ago—that this was what it truly meant to be saved. I genuinely, unquestionably was now saved for eternity. I instantly became free from the bondage of fear, loneliness, selfishness, and much more. I was done living life my way. Not that I was perfect—far from it. But that Lord's Day, I was a new creation in Christ Jesus.

181

God ordained my path—even the future path of severe disabilities. He needed to turn my wheel of faith in the direction of obedience to Him in the late 1960s so that I would be prepared to serve Him in this compromised condition today.

Road of Faith

Before this crossroad of my submission to Christ Jesus back in 1969, my works and plans were either selfish, ambitious, or brought ME praise and accolades, not the Lord. My first thought came early. *I will now live for Him in my words and deeds.* I obediently was baptized at sixteen as an expression of my submission to God.

But like any lifelong commitment, *selfishness* tried to stall my joyous life. Occasionally, I put myself back into the driver's seat and steered slightly off course from time to time. Casual disobedience to God and wrongdoing to others—usually my pride and selfishness—unfortunately, sometimes found its way back on my path. It crept into this new Christian's life much like my car, which had rolled ever so slowly into the intersection's crosswalk while I waited at a red stoplight.

"Christians aren't perfect, just forgiven" is a slogan being thrown around often as a justification for wrongful actions, selfish motives, or wayward thoughts. But, I found that sin brought me no joy.

Instead, I would pull my ride away from the beaten path, stopped at the closest AM/PM quick-mart to refuel my faith. I purchased a beautiful postcard for God and wrote honest words of requested repentance. I stamped it with a prayer, sent my apology via airmail, handed over the keys where God drove us back onto The King's Highway. Once again, back on the correct life course.

I willingly strived—and still do—to be like Jesus day by day. Even throughout my hairpin turns of impairment, I keep on tuning up my faith through ongoing repentance and prayer. I daily fuel my mind and top off my tank by reading or listening to God's Word.

As a Christ-follower, I DO need to set myself apart in my words and my actions. I must treat others differently, so they take notice. Not so others notice me, but so they see my God. No matter what my circumstances, both positive or negative, I trust in God always. He humbles me in my triumphs, and He holds me through my tragedies. I commit to working on showing a selfless, patient attitude. Or rather, I choose to place my attitude, character, demeanor, and temperament into Jesus's hands. His Spirit guides and directs my daily life. God changed me first on the inside, which adjusted my life on the outside.

Choosing Joy

How do others view me as I go through this trial? Am I a kind and upbeat person they want to be around? Or am I *Vicki the Vicious*? I check my motives, attitudes, and behaviors. Two of my favorite quotes from well-known Pastor/Teacher Dr. David Jeremiah are:

"When our lives are filled with peace, faith and joy, people will want to know what we have." [1]

"When I put God first, God takes care of me and energizes me to do what really needs to be done." [2]

Some people are living in a disability crisis like me. Others may be suffering, too—fearful, lonely, confused, or addicted. The list of sufferings we know is endless. Many need or desire a change. I found God will meet and sustain people in and through their crises. If they seek Him, He may be found. If they call, He will answer. If they trust, He is faithful.

In my case, I realized I could not do life on my own. God chose me. I chose to respond. Every minute we all have a choice, don't we? During my trial in the hospitals, I cried out for love, peace, hope, and joy—God's everlasting love, His sweet peace, perfect hope, and pure joy.

So what will life look like for me moving forward? I am not able to change my circumstances, but I am allowed to change my outlook. Will I be helpful or useless? Advantageous, beneficial, constructive—or—disagreeable, discouraging, disinterested? My attitudes may be more crippling than my disabilities. I find that choosing a positive attitude encourages those I come in contact with every hour of every day. Many onlookers are afraid or apprehensive of engaging in conversations until they witness my God-smile and upbeat attitudes.

My pastor—Mike Fabarez—conveys this concept perfectly in his quote, "I will choose to stop complaining & resolve to endure whatever difficulties I may face knowing God will eventually provide relief." [3]

I choose a joyous spirit every day because I never know when that relief may come. I try to put other people's feelings ahead of my own. Humor releases tension and awkwardness around me. It is not all about my comforts or vulnerabilities. It is about making others comfortable and feeling safe. Here is an example:

This summer, Mike, Tiffani, Mike W, Baby Cal, and I were finishing up at a local, hole-in-the-wall taco restaurant. As Tiff carried Cal out the door, a huge barking Husky was directly in our path. Its owner had leashed him to an outside table while he went in to place his order. The dog appeared quite upset, barking at our heels. I casually switched Tiff and the baby away from this danger and put myself smack dab next to this fairly ferocious canine. With a chuckle, I quipped, "Here, Doggy, take a bite of this!" as I stuck out my metal prosthetic leg into his yapping face. Ha! That shut him up quickly as we all laughed and continued to proceed to our cars. I thoroughly enjoy making people laugh.

Transparency also goes a long way in putting strangers at ease as well. When I share my ups and downs, my "thrill of victory and the agony of defeat" [4], others see me as authentic. They see, learn, and know the real me.

Bad News/Good News

Early in my driving career, I received a ticket—excessive speed. I am confident I lost the car privileges for at least a month for that infraction. I went before the Sacramento judge to plead my case, and I had hoped that I did not have to pay a hefty fine. The monetary payment, though, was required for breaking this traffic law. My consequence was to pay the fine or spend time incarcerated. I was not allowed to go to traffic school as I had hoped. I was at a crossroads. I could not afford the payment required by the stern judge, nor did jail look like a punishment I wanted to experience.

All alone in front of the court, I'm embarrassed to say, at 17, I began to cry. The compassionate court mediator informed the judge that he would pay for my ticket. His offer released me of my debt. I was free to go, and I was highly grateful for his act of kindness and mercy. I did not even have enough money to buy him lunch as a thank you gesture!

This experience reminded me of God's ultimate love and sacrifice—*The Story of God's Good News to us.[5-6]*

JUDGE
•God is The Designer, Creator.

•He is Holy and Perfect; I am not.

•Sin separated me from Him.

•Because God is Just, all will stand before Him someday guilty.

PAYMENT OR PENALTY/FINE OR JAIL?
•My payment for sin is death.

•Hell—the consequence—Eternal separation from God.

•My "good deeds" did not earn God's favor as payment for sin.

•Nor can I easily go to a school to expunge my record.

COURT MEDIATOR

•God provided a solution: Jesus—the Mediator between God and man.

•As God, Jesus led the perfect life—He was the perfect sacrifice.

•I had no hope apart from Jesus Christ—He became my substitute.

•Jesus shed his blood, died on the cross, took the punishment I deserved.

•He rose again—conquering death.

RESPONSE?

•Decline payment offered and suffer the consequences (jail) of eternal death and separation from God.

OR...

•Accept the free payment (funds) from Jesus Christ and receive forgiveness from sin, placing total trust in His finished payment on the cross for me.

FREEDOM

•The penalty is paid by Jesus.

•Never to incur the punishment that my sin deserved.

•I received Eternal Life with God.

•God's Holy Spirit—His guarantee—enables believers like me to live a righteous, faithful life.

•The Spirit teaches, guides, comforts, and intercedes for us. [7]

"There is therefore now no condemnation [*blame, judgment*] for those who are in Christ Jesus." Romans 8:1

I found God's Hope and His Joy now that I was forgiven. My payment had been paid. My life was eternally secured.

Love, Hope, and Joy Through Trials

So—What is PERFECT HOPE?

Wishes are based on wants. Hope is longing to have what God promised in His Word. Anticipation easily forms when one eagerly waits to gratify desires or longings like buying a new car or opening a Christmas gift. Hope is patiently waiting on God's timing to receive His good gifts in His perfect time.

Human security is counting on one's own relationships, possessions, good health, or wealth. Hope is relying on God to "...supply every need of yours according to his riches in glory in Christ Jesus." Philippines 4:19

What is PURE JOY, then?

Happiness is derived from earthly means. Joy is given to me from God above. Happiness is temporal, but Joy is eternal. Happiness is situational, yet Joy is constant regardless of circumstances. Happiness is usually a fleeting feeling leaving one desiring more and more. In contrast, Joy is a responsive reaction to God's love and forgiveness, producing contentment.

Even though I lost my hands and feet, I still experience Joy. Although I am not happy about that loss, and it wasn't MY choice, I can still sing God's praises. **But God**...knew this was going to happen to me before the beginning of time. Father God is with me always, no matter what happens. I am dancing on His feet as I hold onto His hands. Jesus fills my heart daily with joy, even throughout extremely tough circumstances. The Holy Spirit comforts and encourages me to keep moving ahead and emboldens me to share God's goodness with others.

I understand my attitude should always be one of thanksgiving. Like I wrote earlier, I often think about my frame of mind and my moods toward others. I can choose to have a bitter countenance and wallow in self-pity (which makes those around me miserable), or I can choose to maintain, instead, a healthy, joyous spirit of an internal Joy.

Quotes for Living a Joyous Life

Like I said earlier, I had the privilege of meeting Ken Tada and Joni Eareckson Tada at the Joni & Friends' Pebble Beach fundraiser event. Way back in the late-1970s—as sophomores at Westmont College in Santa Barbara—Joni spoke in Chapel. The compelling story of her diving accident, paraplegia, and finding salvation through Jesus Christ alone left most of the student body in tears. Joni's personality is warm and inviting. We share not only the common bond of salvation through Christ but also one of many disabilities.

Ken Tada is a strong, courageous man who is caring, kind, and confident. Joni carries herself with such grace and fortitude. The love they share is wonderfully evident to those who are lucky enough to witness this firsthand. Amidst their loving compassion for others, they also bestow God's love toward them even while they deal with Joni's physical limitations, pain, and health crises. Joni's quote regarding God's sovereignty spoke directly to my heart—especially as a quad amputee with my story of loss.

—*"Sometimes God allows what he hates to accomplish what he loves."* [8]

Just the thought of this truth extremely comforts me through my daily fiery trials of disabilities.

"He [God] has chosen not to heal me, but to hold me. The more intense the pain, the closer His embrace."—Joni Eareckson Tada [8].

I found this truth to be genuine in my case as well. I, too, feel God's comforting hugs as I struggle with periodic encounters with pain, mobility and agility difficulties, health trials throughout the day, and my multiple hygiene routines. I am truly grateful for God's demonstrated love and support.

Joni's recent quote found in her September 2020 Joni & Friends' **ministry news** sums up suffering accurately...

"The glory of God is always brighter when he works through the darkest of times." [8]

I concur. During my darkest hours of pain and amputations, God's glory—through His life-miracle for me—was definitely on display for others to see in full force and dazzling radiance! If I were to think of my own quote to define how God sustains me each day, it would be: *"God is either pursuing me through trials or refining me because of them."*

The following suffered greatly through their personal trials. Still, they triumphed: Dietrich Bonhoeffer and Corrie ten Boom (German concentration camps), Joni Eareckson Tada (debilitating spinal cord injury), Nick Vujicic (Born without limbs: *Life Without Limits* [9]), to name a few. Mike and I also had the privilege of listening to Corrie ten Boom speak at Westmont College in the late seventies. We heard Nick share at Saddleback Church to a spell-bound audience. We were glad to have met Nick Vujicic this year, although during a very trying circumstance.

Throughout the centuries, countless have demonstrated God's glory and love for the world to see. I desire to show others the same as I stand holding the trophy on the winner's podium of disabilities. Possibilities are realized through strength and determination. But no more so than through experiencing the love, hope, and joy of the Lord—even while in constant adversity.

Now...

I wish to capture the mind of every reader. I realize that I am not alone in my predicament of pain and loss. Many suffer worse and have been suffering for great lengths of time. Is your 'vehicle' driving through a dark tunnel of adversity, anguish, calamity? Maybe you are experiencing severe discomfort or colossal torment. Or possibly even extreme loss emotionally, physically, spiritually. No one is exempt from pain and difficulty. I am proof positive of that fact.

At any second, a person unknowingly could be about to enter into a season of turbulence—a somewhat *'Twilight Zone''* [10] experience. Life itself presents many crossroads. Decisions must be made quickly and decisively. Truly, it may feel like driving blind in a heavy snowstorm with white-out conditions. One may have no clue which road ahead is the safest one. Which way is up? Which way is down? Do I turn right or left? A terrifying collision may be found right around the bend. **But God...** is All-Knowing. He is the Driver who sees each pothole, rut, and obstacle in the road along the way.

God's Love and Support Through Others

Even though I struggle with limitations throughout my day, God shows me moment by moment that He loves me and is upholding me. I get jazzed when God works all things out for my benefit or sends someone my way to help. He answered my 16-year-old's heart-written prayer by bringing Mike into my life many decades ago. Mike provides for me, prays with me, accomplishes my daily care needs, and encourages me to keep pressing forward.

My Heavenly Father also sustains me through others—my children, grandchildren, family members, friends, pastors, and church family. God is faithful. No matter the trial or situation that I face, faith fuels my engine and mobility—mind, body, and spirit. Are you or a loved one suffering through a devastating health diagnosis, chronic pain, loss of someone you love, destruction or failure of a body part? How about arthritic adversity, feelings of depression or anxiety, countless other hardships, or even found with amputations like me? Faith in God can fuel you, too.

God sees all pain, all suffering, all fiery crashes, and trials.

Our loving Father travels that seemingly unbearable road with those who suffer. He will carry others as He carries me. This highly competent Designated Driver brings a sojourner like me safely to their destination. His Word is truth, and it comforts me. At various times throughout history, God chose the companions of the broken-hearted in body and spirit to carry those daily burdens. Many have done so often in my life.

In addition, I suggest you surround yourself with others for encouragement, assistance, and support. "Brave Battle Buddies," I call them. I have learned throughout my two-year trial that relying on others is not a weakness. There is strength in asking for help. Just be sure to convey thankfulness and gratitude towards them. While you're at it, thank God as well.

As a former first- and second-grade teacher, I loved *"Show and Tell"* time. The students enjoyed it, too. So... 'Show and Tell' these valuable battle warriors precisely what they mean to you, how much you need them, and how much you appreciate and love them. They, too, will desire to discover love, hope, and joy through their caregiving.

Life's Unpredictability, Caution, and Courage

I had no inkling—a couple of years ago—that my God-given, organized, well-managed, mapped-out life was about to be flipped over, twist-turned, topsy-turvy, upside-down. As I looked back to that fear-infused July evening, I felt like my body had been side-swiped by an eighteen-wheeler's tanker filled with an E-Coli infection. This crash was not predicted. I had been extremely healthy three days prior. I had become like a convertible that quickly swerved at the last minute to escape a dangerous rock slide. I strove to overcorrect myself.

In an overly-heightened, highly cautious reaction, my back wheels spun furiously with no traction. This race-car of well-being was out of control. I cascaded over Hwy 50's steep cliff towards death. My once healthy 'vehicle' careened head-long into our frigid, torrential river, which flowed down below our family's cabin.

Medically, I had lost my grip on life's steering wheel. This ejected motorist floundered through the Class 5 rapids and struggled to keep my head above water and stay afloat. For months, I attempted to avoid boulders with razor-sharp scalpels as my body raced toward multiple surgeries. Doctors and nurses worked with lightning speed. How was I to get out of this debilitating problem?

I tried to re-calibrate.

I longed to STOP the turbulent horrors and climb uphill onto the stable, reassuring sandbar. I realized that I could only wrestle the unrelenting waves of surgical rapids for so long before I drowned in self-pity, frustration, and loss.

Instead, I relaxed.

I surrendered my circumstances to God's will and purposes. I was only anchored physically through Jesus Christ's redemptive plan and miraculous works. With Jesus's firm grip of my hand through adversity, He pulled not only my body but also my life and my soul to safety. I found normalcy, rest, and serenity on that peaceful riverbank. I was safe and sound—though badly bruised and battered—as I laid in His loving arms.

After I was deemed "out of the woods," I was especially interested to hear others' viewpoints of my predicament. I was not lucid during the vast majority of my trip. So, I requested many family members and friends to fill me in via e-mails. *(See Chapter 9.)* That way, I could refer back anytime to each memo or letter for guaranteed love, support, and strength through my difficult times of functionality and Rehabilitation. I will continue to be encouraged by God through remembrance and knowledge since I was there in body and spirit, even though not in mind.

"To God be the glory, great things He has done!" [11]

Let's spend quality time together and tour more slowly, confidently through the precious promises and assurances I found throughout my entire pilgrimage.

BUT GOD...

"And Jesus answered them, 'Have faith in God.'" Mark 11:22

"And he [Jesus] said to the woman, 'Your faith has saved you; go in peace.'" Luke 7:50

Check this out...

"What is the Gospel" on you.tube.com (Mike Fabarez/focalpointministries.org) [12]

Moving Week

CHAPTER 8

PRECIOUS PILGRIMAGE

"You were wearied with the length of your way, but you did not say, 'It is hopeless'; you found new life for your strength, and so you were not faint." Isaiah 57:10

As I finalized my journey to discover love, hope, and joy, the most central theme was to have God as my benefactor. He provided for me many things, but these were the top five I realized along this journey:

1) **Heartfelt** change from God's invitation for 'A New Life' in Christ.
2) **History** with my family, church, and friends.
3) **His healing** miracle on my behalf.
4) **Health**, strength, and mobility were regained.
5) **Hardcore** pain and effort to complete God's future assignments.

To finish a strong race, I required all five actions going into the final lap. If one of these critical elements were missing, I would have spun out, flipped over, and stalled. God knew what I needed every mile of this journey. He controlled my roadster until the checkered flag waved. My Father continually fueled my faith through multiple trials, turbulence, and trauma. He brought me to a secure and safe road while He granted me the soundness of my mind, body, and spirit. Through these fabulous five-mile markers, life produced joy for my present today and hope for my future tomorrow.

Life is a funny thing. I never quite realized that my life on earth could end in a flash. My brain didn't compute that fact frequently enough. I believed if I had thought about my mortality more often, I would have thanked God for many more precious moments throughout my life. I wondered—pre-illness— *Did I have a "close call" today and didn't realize it?*

A few times in childhood, I could—or possibly should—have died early on in life. Once, I fell through a plastic inner-tube floaty in a crowded swimming pool. And as a toddler—unable to swim—I descended under the surface. I sunk like a car driven into a pristine lake by mistake. Or a vehicle sunk in a deep ravine's floodwaters during an intense hurricane. I eagerly awaited rescue in the calmest way. I could have drowned, but I didn't.

Another time, if I had followed my mother and baby sister as they crossed the street while we Trick-or-Treated, I would have been hit by that speeding VW as it whipped around our neighborhood corner. I could have died, but I didn't.

As a new driver, an old car I drove suddenly croaked in the middle of the road in front of on-coming traffic as I attempted to make a left turn. I could have been fatally struck, but I wasn't.

Additionally, while I was on a date, my companion—after a split-second decision—avoided a hazardous rear-end car accident. We had been casually talking while we waited at a red light. My date just happened to view this careless driver in his rearview mirror just in time to shift his car over to get far out of his way. *Vroom!* A drunk driver in his speeding vehicle ran the red light straight through the intersection at a very high rate of speed. Cops pursued. We would have been smashed from behind, but we weren't.

Once again, the most horrific experience of my life was as I laid in various hospital beds a couple of years ago and suffered from septic shock. My uncountable tubes, IV equipment, and monitors were attached everywhere. I know I should have died, but again I didn't.

Thank you, God, for another precious day that You have ordained for me.

Individual existence sometimes is very fragile indeed. A friend recently discovered this fact as well. Death may occur at any age, in any way, during any time, at any place.

Recently, her daughter-in-law was severely T-boned by another driver who ran a red light traveling at speeds of approximately 60+mph. After her vehicle was struck on the passenger side in the middle of her right-of-way intersection, it flipped before landing on its top with considerable damage. A witness had to break out the back window before he pulled her to safety. She was only moderately injured. She was sore and tender for about a week. By the grace of God, her two young children—toddler and newborn, both girls—were not in the backseat traveling with her as usual. The infant baby belted into her car seat would have been in the direct path of impact from that speeding car. Tragic loss of lives would have occurred within seconds! But they didn't.

This same friend also witnessed her daughter rescue her nine-year-old grandson trapped in the strong Pacific Ocean's gripping riptide. As beach-goers saw this drama unfold, many asked her if their family needed any assistance. No lifeguards were on duty at the time. My friend replied, "I don't believe so because she is a trained lifeguard and teaches swimming lessons." Upon hearing that positive news, onlookers relaxed and let it play out with excellent results. Even though she had many years of water safety training, this young mom conveyed just how difficult it became to save her son. But within moments—after abundant caution, warnings, and a riptide tutorial from his mother—he frolicked once again in the cool, pleasurable ocean waves. He should have drowned, but he didn't.

"I could have lost half of my family last week!" this girlfriend told us these events at dinner one night. She was correct. It was more likely than not. But we all believe God is in control. Sovereign. Life and death are held in His hands. He is the giver and taker of life itself.

In scripture, David pleaded, "Turn, O LORD, deliver my life; save me for the sake of your steadfast love." Psalm 6:4

Some asked me gently, "Have you ever wished you would have somehow died and gone to heaven?" No. I think instead, *What do I have left to offer*

God that He wants to use? Or what does He want me to accomplish using the remainder of my life? That realization to me is a HUGE responsibility. I don't want to waste any more precious time.

I connect strongly with Noah Ray's blog words on this subject,

"How many days do I have left? I don't know. No one does, except God. He knows the exact number of years, days, hours and seconds that I will occupy my address on Planet Earth; the exact moment that my death will occur." [1]

Death for me should have arrived anytime between July 6th and mid-July for sure. Any one of my medical conditions with each of my failing internal organs could have taken away my last breath. Many trauma professionals told Mike and me I was lucky to be alive. Miracle milestones along the way were spectacular, of which to be a part. I know it was not luck that brought me through this fiery trial. It was God's plan all along. He was not surprised or shocked. It was God Who chose life for me.

~*~

I reflect on His gracious love as He drove, inspired, and encouraged me during our treacherous travels together. I was—in the passenger seat—secure through His multiple promises.

God's Promises

As His child, I realized through everything thrown my way...

- He is always with me no matter what.
- He is always in control of every situation.
- He has granted to me all things that pertain to life and godliness.
- He is always good and gives perfect gifts.

- He is my strength, my protector, and my provider.

I enjoyed abundant benefits and promises during this trying time. I sought virtues to supplement my faith because I needed everything that God offered me—Virtue, Knowledge, Self-Control, Steadfastness, Godliness, Brotherly Affection, Love. (See: 2 Peter 1:3-8.) Five more benefits I additionally gleaned were added: Peace, Patience, Strength, Fortitude, and Perseverance.

God's Assurances

But God also promises the full assurance of hope.

Hebrews 6:11-12..."And we desire each one of you to show the same earnestness to have the full assurance of hope until the end, so that you might not be sluggish, but imitators of those who through faith and patience inherit the promises."

Love, hope, and joy were found along my precious journey. How can I say 'precious' at all? Wasn't this race precarious, not precious? It was, indeed, both—precarious physically, yet precious mentally and spiritually. God, through His eternal love, gave me confident hope and comforting joy. Love, hope, and joy were equally found in God and His attributes:

God is Infinite, Unchanging, Self-Sufficient. All-Powerful, All-Knowing, Omnipresent. Fully Wise and Knowledgable, Faithful and True. Good, Just, Merciful, Gracious. Loving, Holy, Great, and Glorious. [2]

I fell deeper in love with God, my first love, through my adversity and challenges.

How does anyone find out how strong or resilient they are or will become until they are put to the test? Until they are refined by fire? Or extreme heat and pressure are applied? It resembles in my mind "test crashes." How do manufacturers know a new prototype vehicle measures up to safety standards? They test them in multiple "crash" situations. How do those who race realize they have a winning car? They test it out on the track *well before* entering the race. Who competes if they know they cannot win?

Put through many extreme tests—physically, spiritually, and mentally—I survived each one. Toxins and infections were burning me from the inside out. Debilitating pressures almost squeezed the life right out of me.

Challenges ensued. I knew no matter what, I was not to give up or check out while I laid paralyzed in bed. Pressures that produced discouragement loomed over my "new look" and my inability to function as skillfully as I had before. Disqualification from further competing in my race to the finish line could have side-lined me. But, severe testing only brought out a competitive, God-spirit within me. Because of these extreme fire-testings, I grew stronger in my faith, more powerful in my mind, and tenacious in my body.

Also, this intense heat and powerful pressures proved in me genuine faith, spiritual endurance, biblical stability, and safety through positive relationships. Not because of me, but because of God. I am not capable of that strength and power. **But God**... Jesus looked at them and said, "With man it is impossible, but not with God. For all things are possible with God." Mark 10:27.

I know now that I can face more each hour if I grasp that I cannot accomplish life on my strength and reliability. God has refined me into something precious and beautiful. Both God and my incredible husband are right beside me every step of the way, gassing my tank, fueling my faith, and racing me forward throughout this life.

The fact remains that this race was in preparation for the next. Then that win will solidify and strengthen me for another. Someday soon, I may complete my last race here on earth—the final checkered flag and my last trophy. Only God knows when the final beat of my heart will occur. Therefore, I will continue to compete until then. Just for the record, I race to WIN!

"In this you rejoice, though now for a little while, if necessary, you have been grieved by various trials, so that the tested genuineness of your faith—more precious than gold that perishes though it is **tested by fire**—may be found to result in **praise** and **glory** and **honor** at the revelation of Jesus Christ." 1 Peter 1:6-7.

Tested by fire!

Not only did I lose my feet, but also both my hands. Yet, throughout this debilitating ordeal, I knew God was redirecting my steps from now on. My strong faith in Jesus Christ is my dashboard of stability and the compass that guides me on my travels. I found not only love but hope and joy as well. Even small victories were celebrated on my God-mapped journey throughout life. I won my race, because God was the One driving.

Before illness struck, life—for both of us—was spent traveling through each minute at warp speed. Accomplishing much, but not necessarily enjoying the finer things along the journey. We now slow down and maintain our speed on cruise control. I immensely appreciate God's smooth excursion of comfort, faith, guidance, and especially love. I like the idea that my niece, Noelle, has shared with family...

> *"Make sure to not speed through life in too big of a hurry. Make sure to enjoy 'The Journey' along the way!"* [3]

My upcoming course is still being maneuvered by the mighty hand of God. He has truly become—no doubt—my hands and feet. He continuously fuels my faith, no matter what challenges arise. I have long discovered love, hope, and joy along God's winning path called "The Game of Life!®.□"

~*~

After I turned 60 years old, my world—as I knew it—was forever altered. I had gone through this horrific tragedy one fateful July day. My body was perfectly healthy and whole on the 4th. But by July 7th, I was found on death's door. This September 1st marked the second anniversary of the amputation loss of my hands and feet. My life has never been the same since my milestone birthday. But that's okay. Even though I have been *tested by fire,* I am confidently assured that I am—and always will be—unwaveringly *fueled by faith.* I trust God Almighty with my whole life—Past, Present, and Future!

"RACE TO WIN!"

My Faithful God

God has made me who I am
He has promised life anew
God will travel as my guide
He will bring me through.

—Vicki Zoradi

BUT GOD...

"I know that you can do all things, and that no purpose of yours can be thwarted." Job 42:2

"You have turned for me my mourning into dancing; you have loosed my sackcloth and clothed me with gladness, that my glory may sing your praise and not be silent. O LORD my God, I will give thanks to you forever!" Psalm 30:11-12

Check out videos, pod-casts, additional photos, and

"The Vicki Zoradi Story" at: vickizoradi.com

@vickizoradi #vickizoradi
@Quad4God #Quad4God

Follow Vicki on Facebook, Instagram and Twitter

Kyburz Cabin—Summer 2020

Contact Vicki at vickizoradi@gmail.com

CHAPTER 9

PERSPECTIVES FROM FAMILY & FRIENDS

"The heart of her husband trusts in her, and he will have no lack of gain."
Proverbs 31:11

"Grandchildren are the crown of the aged, and the glory of children is their fathers." Proverbs17:6

"But your friends be like the sun as he rises in his might." Judges 5:31b

I wish to introduce my incredible family, friends, colleagues, and church family through their thoughts during my situation. For the most part, I was comatose through their experiences, so I highly value their perspectives. The following thoughts and reflections they each shared made me weep. I felt blessed, like I was there with them, embracing each one during my tragic moments. I believe you will be shocked at the love and commitment, strength, and tenacity in which my loved ones looked at our circumstances and situations. I was extremely humbled and impressed as I read them a year after my horrific journey had begun. Please sit back and celebrate with me these *unedited* memories.[1]

My Dear Precious Wife,

I love you. Here is my perspective...

There were several major takeaways from Vicki's near death experience. Starting with her ER doctor, who within minutes of our arrival to Marshall hospital, told my daughter Tiffani and me that Vicki's current condition upon arrival was life threatening. That sent chills over my body as I considered what went wrong so fast. I wasn't at all prepared for that shocking news. I quickly realized this medical outcome was in the hands of my Great Physician, Jesus Christ.

In that very moment, God put on my heart the Bible verse in James 5:16b which says, "The prayer of a righteous person has great power as it is working." God had graciously given me that verse to memorize just weeks before this incident.

As Vicki struggled to survive with four nurses and doctors around her bed administering IVs for fluid resuscitation and antibiotics, I quickly realized the need to get thousands of believers praying for her. This would be critical. Also, I wanted God to know my trust was in HIM! After many calls, texts, and e-mails for immediate prayers, within hours an army of believers were fervently praying for us.

Secondly, God revealed to me that this circumstance was all about HIM being glorified as described by the Lord himself in John 9:1-3 with the blind man. Jesus' disciples asked him in verse 2, "Rabbi, who sinned, this man or his parents, that he was born blind." Jesus replied that neither was true. He added in scripture, "...but that the works of God might be displayed in him."(verse 3) WOW, what a revelation to me!

Third, God provided me the peace that passes all understanding described in Philippians 4:7. Only by the power of the Holy Spirit would that be possible as my wife of 40 years and the most precious human being on the planet to me was on death's doorstep.

God gave me unexplainable peace that when the doctors said no that God could step in and say yes. Even during the darkest hours with no measurable blood pressure, I knew my sovereign God was in control. I had never felt this kind of peace in such desperate conditions…amazing.

This experience was very helpful because a few weeks later the vascular surgeon told me that Vicki's limbs were unable to be saved due to a lack of blood flow. As I left the hospital that night, I was broken hearted and wept on the way to my car. God gave me me two things that day that provided that same peace that passes all understanding.

An unexpected text came in from a friend that had experienced a lot of medically related issues. He said, "Many times recovery is two steps forward and one step back. Don't get too down during the bad days." Just what the doctor ordered!

That same night, God gave me a dream that made the events of that day all so clear…

Vicki and I were in the grocery store when a lady had noticed Vicki's prosthetic hands. Vicki asked the lady if she wanted to hear her story and she said, "Certainly." Vicki proceeded to tell her story and eventually shared her faith and the gospel to her. That's when the light went off in my head. I realized this tragedy was about the eternal not the temporal.

My last takeaway was the need to be connected to family and the fellowship of believers. Both Vicki and I realized family members were 'there for us' during the first hours and up to a year later in ways too great for words. I'm so grateful we had them in our lives and praise God for their commitment to us. Also, we were involved in several ministries and bible studies at Compass Bible Church when this tragedy occurred and the support we received from the body of Christ was priceless. Lastly, we have many long term friendships and more recent ones where the love they poured into us was humbling.

Love you,

Mike (My Wonderful Husband of 41 years, Love of My Life, Spiritual Leader, Confidante, Healthcare Advocate and Daily Caregiver, Prayer Warrior)

Hey Mom, [Son David]

In the summer of 2018, I found that I had never emotionally prepared for the dreaded phone call in the middle of the night from a loved one to let me know about a tragedy that had taken place. Looking back years afterwards, I realized it was not something I prepared for in any relationship, let alone a parent. Yet the night of July 6th at 2am is exactly when that happened, where I received a call from my sister to tell me our mother was fighting for her life.

We knew Mom had been having health issues with some kidney stones and had been praying for her from afar as we live two states away; but to have talked to her the day before on her happy 60th birthday and hearing that she was doing fine, that phone call came as a complete shock. Our prayers in that moment went from having the Lord help her recover from the kidney stones to begging through tears of confusion for the Holy Spirit to spare her life.

My wife and I got a few hours sleep, then packed our car and our 9 month old boy and drove through the night to be there as quickly as we could. In those hours spent driving, singing praise and worship songs and in a constant state of prayer, my wife and I realized that the Holy Spirit was moving. There was a plan, we just had no idea what that was going to be.

Information being relayed from family members about what was taking place and Mom's condition could only go so far. It wasn't until we arrived there in the small, little hospital in Placerville, California did we realize just how severe septic shock could be. In just the few hours since we first saw her, we were left in helplessness as we watched Mom deteriorate in front of our eyes. All we were left with was getting to say our goodbyes and continued prayers for the healing power of Jesus to somehow work a Lazarus-sized miracle.

That night was one of the most profound nights of my life. My wife, who is a gifted worship leader queued up songs of praise and lead our family in the tiny little waiting room in one of the most beautiful worship sessions I have ever been a part of. Time stood still while we worshipped, prayed, petitioned for the Kingdom of Heaven to intervene. That night we caught a small glimpse of what it would be like to stand in the presence of the Almighty God in surrendered worship.

The next morning was when everything changed. Dad and I had slept in the waiting room that night to give my sister and brother-in-law a chance to get some sleep in a bed. It wasn't until around 6 in the morning did we go in to discover that rather than getting worse, Mom started to get better. Her heart was stronger. Her vital organs were getting the blood supply they needed.

Over the next few weeks, hour by hour updates and miracle after miracle, Mom was recovering. It wasn't until she woke up, was able to open her eyes and look at me, my wife and her grandson did it fully hit me what the Lord had done. Little then did we know the full extent of what the Lord had in store for our Mother. After months and months in the ICU and quadruple amputations, did we start to see that God healed Mom for a very specific purpose. She is with us today as a testimony, not only to the power and love of God, but to also provide hope. Mom is a perfect example of what it means to pick up your cross daily and follow Jesus. She wakes up and with Dad's help puts on her prosthetic arms and legs to live and radiate the love of God. Vicki Zoradi is the strongest, bravest and most inspiring person I have the pleasure of knowing and get the honor of being able to call her my Mother.

Love you so much,

David (Loving Son, Resides with Keana and kids in Vancouver, WA.— Wish his family lived closer, Prayer Warrior)

[Daughter-In-Love Keana]

There are moments in life that are etched into memory forever. The early morning of July 6, 2018 is one of those moments for me. I will never forget the phone call that changed our lives, as Dave talked to Tiffani and we heard a frantic, terrified voice repeating "Mom is dying." How could that be? We just sang happy birthday to her yesterday?

As our little family spun through the following hours packing in a daze, trying to make sure we had everything we needed for our drive from Washington to California—we would pause every once in a while overwhelmed with the reality that Mom's body was fighting to survive. We would pray, receive visions from the Lord of His army at her doorstep, seeing into the battle that is not of this world. The flesh and blood of Vicki Zoradi was experiencing the reality of a spiritual fight for her body.

When we arrived to California, we brought with us one of the brightest joys of Vicki's life—Jet—her 9 month old grandson. I will never forget seeing her light up when she saw him. She couldn't speak, and was barely still with us cognitively, but it was clear that she was so happy. The next few hours and days brought our family into the lowest of lows. A transfer to a bigger hospital, new therapy and drugs to keep her organs alive, and a team of doctors doing their best to keep her going.

In the middle of one of the hardest moments of our lives, the Holy Spirit was alive and active. Moving in the body of believers up and down the west coast, petitioning for a miracle. One night our extended family had taken over the ICU waiting room, and we had an incredible time of worship, praising our Maker and surrendering ourselves and Vicki to Him. Faith was emboldened, courage was increased, and yet Vicki continued to worsen.

Jesus on the cross is the clearest picture of sorrow and hope all contained into a single moment. We experienced the deepest sorrow when the doctor explained to Dad and us kids that there was nothing left they could do to try and save Vicki's body. That her heart wouldn't be able to maintain the stress of this sickness for much longer, and that it was time to start saying goodbye. Yet, we had hope. We had hope for healing and peace over her, knowing she would be at rest and eternal communion with our Savior. After hours and hours of weeping, praying, talking to her and singing—Mom's body hung on. To defy all odds, medicine, and the mind of man, Mom's condition shifted. Her organs started to revive. In a modern day Ezekiel moment, where there was no more life, God breathed it back in.

Vicki Zoradi is a walking picture of the hope we have in Jesus. That His Holy Spirit is alive and active in us. Sickness and brokenness is not the heart of our Father, and yet He has taken what the enemy meant to rip apart and destroy, to be a light on the hill for His glory. Jesus has overcome evil once again—and the kingdom of God is empowered through the miracle that is my mother-in-law. What an honor it is to have her in my life, and I will be forever grateful that my kids will grow up with Nana, and not just stories of her. I will end with this: "May the God of hope fill you with all joy and peace as you trust in him, so that you may overflow with hope by the power of the Holy Spirit" - Romans 15:13. Let it be Lord, and may we all hold onto the hope that is promised to us through His Spirit.

- Keana Zoradi (Loving Daughter-In-Law, Beautiful Spiritual Heart for God, Fantastic Prayer Warrior)

Mom's Story/My Memories, [Tiffani]

Earth shattering. That's how I felt when I first heard the words that my mommy's hospital visit was "life threatening." How? She was talking to me just five minutes ago. I felt like I was not living in reality. Memories flood my heart of us listening to oldies music in our backyard as we sang along and floated in the pool back when I was a teenager. I was preparing for the worst but begging God, "Please don't take her."

The Miracle Tuesday, as we all called it, was also another out of the body experience. When I got the phone call at 5am, I was so scared to answer. I thought...The one night I don't sleep at the hospital of course she passes. Guilt came rushing in. I'll never forget that joyous phone call. I cried the happiest tears of my life. I've never praised God with more zeal in my soul, besides my salvation day!

Watching Mom come back to life before our eyes was the biggest pleasure. I got to have a privileged role of caring for her. It was hard seeing her so helpless at times. BUT her joy made my relationship with her, Christ and my family so much stronger. Some of my favorite memories were waking up at 2am to my mom asking for ice chips at the hospital. I loved that she needed me to help her. I loved that I could somehow be that safe place for her and that she trusted me. More importantly she trusted the Lord.

Once I got pregnant (after infertility), my mom was my biggest supporter. I was pregnant while she was going through the rehab process! She prayed for my son so much and we had the best time together.

I absolutely love what God is doing in and through my mother. The lessons I learned:

1. God is always in control 100% (I knew this, but I truly experienced it in a huge way). We can trust Him to do what will bring Him glory and whatever He does will be for our good in the end (Romans 8:28)

2. My mom is a living example of the gospel on display.

3. Prayer is crucial. It is crucial that God's people are living the Christian life in obedience to Christ.

Tiffani Washburn (Loving Daughter, My Occupational and Physical Therapist, Excellent Caregiver, Prayer Requests Pusher, Prayer Warrior)

[Son-In-Love Mike W's reflections]

In the summer and fall of 2018, my mother-in-law, Vicki Zoradi, entered into a trial that the vast majority of the world has never experienced or ever will. To the world, they may say her story is such a pity; so awful that something so tragic could happen to one person. But you won't hear that from her. Vicki has embraced her trials and sufferings as a unique and opportune way to glorify Christ and tell others about the wonderful works of God. Of course it hasn't been easy—but it has been worth it.

Being at death's door, suffering in the ICU for 40+ days, losing her hands and her feet, adapting to the struggles of everyday life as a quadrilateral amputee: these were and still are all things which grew her character and stretched her faith in God. Trials that 1 Peter 1:7 were brought "so that the tested genuineness of your faith—more precious than gold that perishes though tested by fire—may be found to result in praise and glory and honor at the revelation of Jesus Christ." I do not know any other person that has lived this verse so well.

I knew it was serious when Mike, Vicki's husband, came from the ER room where we had just taken Vicki in Placerville, and broke down in tears after the doctor has just told him that her condition was "life threatening." "How can this be?" I thought to myself. We had just spent the previous day celebrating her 60th birthday party at the family cabin near Lake Tahoe. Our Nana, who beamed with bright smiles and big blue eyes the day before, was battling for her life from a lodged kidney stone that had caused her to go into severe septic shock. Outside of the ER, Dad composed himself, took Tiffani and I by the hands, and said "We need to pray."

What began there that Friday evening, with loud cries and supplications, carried on through the weekend and into the early hours of the next week. Vicki's condition worsened over that time period, to the point where the doctors at the new hospital in Sacramento had encouraged us to say our goodbyes to Mom Monday evening. The doctors felt firm in their prognosis that Mom would pass away that night, but God had other plans.

I had never known what it looked like to "pour out your heart to God" until I was around the Zoradi family for those long days and nights in the ICU. Led by Mike and accompanied by multiple family members, we all prayed harder than we had ever prayed before in our lives. When we weren't praying, we were singing loud hymns and worship songs in the family waiting room that we had taken over (peacefully of course). God granted us the faith that carried us through, and ultimately God spared Mom's life. It was nothing short of a miracle—an undeniable fact that even one of our atheist nurses was bewildered by.

Vicki's story is an example of immense suffering, but even greater grace and love poured out by God. The Lord has strengthened her every step of the way, and he continues to get glory from her story from the people she shares with. What is an even more incredible aspect of her story—one that she'll never tell—is that fact that I've never once heard her complain or ask "why me?" She's an amazing example of trusting in God when things don't go the way that we would have planned.

With love,

Mike Washburn (Loving Son-in-law, Jesus' Miracles & Psalms Scripture Reader, Great Treat Giver! Encourager, Prayer Warrior)

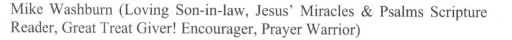

[Dad] I entered the hospital as the elder of the group. Those that were standing in the waiting room were my son Mike and his wife Brenda, my granddaughter Michelle, my daughter Valori and her husband Paul, my grandson Ryan and his wife Rachel, granddaughters Noelle, Tiffani and her husband Mike, grandson David and his wife Keana, great-grandchild Jet, and many others. Son-in-law, Mike Zoradi, was with my daughter Vicki as she was laying in the hospital bed fighting between life and death. We all were there asking God to please spare her life. I was a proud father, grandfather and great-grandfather for the Christian legacy that has been passed down to those that love the Lord and were praying. I thought of so many families that don't have that same 'prayer power' we had that week. I know that Vicki's mother was looking down from above and was just as happy that we were praying for Vic. God answered our prayers!

Love, Dad (Bill Patterson, 90-year-old, who resided in Sacramento, currently lives with his children, Daily Prayer Warrior)

[Brother Mike and His Wife Brenda]

Vicki, I apologize for the length of this but walking through this journey with you has been overwhelmingly humbling and you have been such an example to Bren and me of God's incredible grace and your beautiful spirit. We pray that God continues to lift you up by His mighty right hand and use you for His glory in magnificent ways. I'm not completely sure what you are planning with this, but I hope that reading it brings you joy and no tough memories. We hope it helps. Bren and I love you so much!

Reflections:

I can remember receiving the desperate call from my Brother-in-law like it happened yesterday. Any call received in the middle of the night brings an immediate level of concern and the look on Brenda's face as she answered the phone and listened was enough to confirm that something really bad was unfolding. The conversation concluded, she filled me in and we launched into "urgency" mode, throwing some clothes in the car and heading to Placerville, CA...knowing that my sister "might not survive the night." While bewildered and confused (Vicki is so young and healthy), we were not in disbelief or total shock because we have experienced real tragedy and shocking news in our own lives and we know that bad things can and do happen to good people. We arrived about nine hours later to find Vicki in a hospital bed, struggling for her life. She knew we were there, but it was clear that this was an incredibly serious and life threatening situation. Over the next several hours and into the following morning, we prayed hard, held on to hope and to each other as Mike was required to make extremely serious and consequential decisions over Vicki's care. The details of Vicki's remarkable story have been (and will continue to be) told so my desire here is to provide details of the profound impact her journey has had on Brenda and me jointly and on me personally.

This journey that God took Brenda and me through together was profound in many respects. Rarely, in the human experience, are people thrust so abruptly into a protracted roller coaster ride of emotions as we were. At once, we were experiencing the potential tragic loss of someone who we loved so much and to whom we were so close and a flood of familiar emotions from a tragedy that we had experienced so many years earlier. We understood that we were fully engaged in a support role with my sister's husband Mike. While the word "fervently" does not seem an adequate description for what we were engaged in, we prayed fervently together, most often through tears. We desperately wanted God's sovereign will to align with our desires. Brenda and I both grew up in very conservative, non-charismatic Christian families. As such, when as a larger group we were pouring out our hearts to God for Vicki's life...viscerally, vocally and loudly in a chaotic and non-structured way, we experienced the presence of God our Father and a unity of Believers like we have never experienced before...it was profound and powerful. When the doctor's informed Mike that everything had been done and the end was very near for Vicki, our begging and imploring turned to praise for her life and what she has meant to all of us. Then Mike, no doubt led by the Spirit, emphatically asked us all if we would all still love and trust in God if his answer to our individual and collective prayers was "No." We were all in surrender...God was on the throne and would stay there...a powerful moment.

God, in His incredible mercy performed a miracle before our very eyes. He saved my sister, that I love so much. My personal journey has led me to a place where my worship has been freed from a critical spirit. By this experience, I have drawn closer to my God which I have known my entire life and accepted at age ten. For me has been a little like waking from a slumber to discover that there is a deeper relationship with the LORD available that I have kept just out of arm's length or perhaps something I didn't desire at all believing it to be non-essential. My relative apathy, kept me from tremendous joy and fulfillment. One simple example is that my otherwise "hands in pocket" approach to worshipping in church has been untethered and released to allow my hands and voice to be raised to Him in praise and adoration. The freedom I experience when I do so often brings me to tears in humble joy and thankfulness for what my Father has done for me. It has been a personal rebirth in many ways. The LORD has given Vicki such a supernatural joy through such a profound loss that every time we are together she is a living testimony to God's grace, mercy and love. It pours out of her and it is infectious. When we are together, I am immediately drawn closer to Him...everyone that experiences her remarkably deep and genuine joy experiences the same. I am honored to be her favorite (only) brother and to be walking with her as a small part of her journey.

Love to you, Vicki.

Your favorite brother and sister-in-law,

Mike and Brenda Patterson (My Loving Brother and Sister-in-law who reside in Fallbrook, California. Our 'rocks' during this entire trial—"Whatever You Need Physically, Mentally, Spiritually, we will be there for you both!" Prayer Partners)

[Sister Valori and her husband Paul]

Our perspective...

We left our family cabin at 8pm where we had spent the day with the family hoping to celebrate my sister's 60th birthday. Unfortunately, she was feeling ill and we were unable to celebrate with her. At around 1am, the phone rang and I got up to answer it. It was my Brother-in-law Mike Z telling me that they had taken Vicki back to the hospital and that she had Septic Shock and may not make it. I remember not comprehending what he was saying as I was in a deep sleep prior to the phone call. Mike repeated it again and then Tiffani their daughter said, "Aunt Val, this is serious." I don't even remember how the phone call ended, but I remember going back to bed telling my husband Paul what was happening. He held me as I was shaking uncontrollably.

We got up and dressed and headed to Placerville's Hospital. When we arrived, Mike, Tiffani and Tiffani's husband Mike W, were sitting around her bed and I remember the doctor coming in and saying that they had given her meds (Vasopressors) to protect her organs and had put a stent into her kidneys to remove the blockage. At that point she was on a ventilator but was awake and waving. We hugged her and sat with her in her room. Over the next few hours my husband Paul and I took turns with the family staying with her. She was asleep most of that time or was in a drug-induced coma, I'm not sure. By morning, when all looked stable, Paul and I left to go rest before doing an airport run. We headed back to the hospital with our daughter and their niece, Noelle, who we had just picked up and saw that our brother Mike P. (Too many Mike's in this family!) and his wife Brenda had arrived after driving all night from Southern California. At this point, other family members were arriving as well.

Sometime in the early afternoon, we were told that because of her kidneys, she needed continuous dialysis and they were not set up for that there in Placerville. They said she wouldn't make it if they didn't get her transferred to the Sacramento hospital and that she may not make it during transport. We waited outside of Placerville hospital waiting to see Vicki go by ambulance and praying for her to survive the trip. We followed shortly behind.

After arriving at Sutter Hospital, we all went to the "family waiting room." I remember the orderlies quickly bringing her in and were bumping her bed into doorways and there was a lot of shouts of orders being carried out as they were wheeling her to do another stent procedure. I remember her nurse, "Amy" coming into the family room area telling us that Vicki was very ill and the most critical patient in their hospital. She explained about the procedure Vicki was having done (another stent and trying to remove the large stone). Then she said something we all didn't understand at the time about her "graying effect" and that it would be explained later after they got her stabilized. The "graying effect" ended up being her extremities losing circulation due to the pressor meds they gave her to send all the blood to her organs to keep them alive. This caused her hands and feet to turn gray and then eventually black.

Things took a turn for the worse the next day and by Monday, the docs said there was nothing else they could do. I will never forget the time we all spent around her bed saying how much we loved her, said our goodbyes, and the beautiful hymns that we sung in her room that day. When we finished, I remember going back in the family room where Mike Z asked the whole family if we were all ok to let Vicki go and give her to the Lord. We all agreed and we prayed like never before and you could feel the Presence of the Lord in that room. Sometime during the night (wee early morning of Tuesday), she turned a corner and came back to us! We got our miracle! God was so faithful.

The day she woke up from her induced coma was such an exciting day! To see her awake after thinking we had lost her was amazing! She was asked some questions by the nurse and asked to respond by raising her eyebrows (she was still on the ventilator at this point). She responded to the questions asked and it appeared that there was no brain damage from the Sepsis. What a miracle!

However, each day brought its hurdles, and everyday a different specialist would tell Mike that they were concerned with one of her organs. Mike would sit in on the doctor's briefing for Vicki and he asked what it was they would like to see happen in her numbers whether going up or down in certain blood counts. He would come back and tell us how we should pray (and always sent a text to their church prayer team back home) and we would gather around and pray specifically for that number to reach what it needed to reach that day. It seemed one by one as we prayed, each number would get to where it needed to be! God again was so faithful.

Throughout her stay, Vicki was a trooper. She never complained once. I never saw her down or cry. Poor thing, she had so many procedures done during her hospital stay, that every night she would ask Mike if she was going to be having any procedures the next day, but she never broke down or got discouraged. She truly is an amazing person! I believe that God in his mercy, gave her the will, strength and attitude she needed to get through her ordeal. Only God could've done that. It's not humanly possible to go through what she went through and not complain.

One day that really sticks out in my mind, was right before Vicki's transport from the Sacramento hospital to Southern California. Mike Z told Paul and I and Mike and Brenda that it was possible that she was going to be losing both her hands and her feet. This was so devastating to us. We all hugged and cried and prayed for protection of Vicki's mind to be free of depression and anger over this news. Later, Mike had a dream at night where Vicki was a quad amputee, and she was sharing her story with a stranger in a store and giving God the glory!

Even during the days leading up to her amputations when you would think it would be a devastating, depressing time, I remember her telling us, "Why would I want these hands and feet that are all shriveled up and black?" And later when facing her amputation surgery, she told me the vision God had given her, of her as a little girl dancing on the feet of God her Father and Him saying, "I will be your hands and feet!" Wow! God is so good!

I am convinced that throughout Vicki's ordeal, our All-Knowing God who knew what was going to happen from the beginning of time, sent her who she was going to need at such a time as this. God placed them in her life long before she needed them! God gave her a husband who is a hands-on caregiver and who never once complains or gets frustrated, a daughter who is an Occupational Therapist who moved into Vicki and Mike's home along with her husband to help with her therapy during her recovery, a son-in-law Mike W who is an amazing servant and was there through it all doing whatever was needed. They were Vicki's support during her year-long recovery. Lastly, God sent a guy from their church that owns a prosthetic office and was a huge blessing in Vicki's mobility recovery. They all came together like pieces of a puzzle so that Vicki got the help she needed to survive and thrive! So together, her and Mike have a story and ministry that they can share to anyone and everyone while lifting up the name of the Lord!

This to me, is a story of a merciful God who heard the anguished prayers of His children and chose to answer our prayers and heal my sister and give her back to us.

Love you forever Sis!

Valori and Paul Parks (Our much loved sister & brother-in-law from Lincoln, California in 2018, moved to Coeur D' Alene, ID in 2019. Mike's anchor in the first two months. His home away from home. Visited often in Southern California. Prayer Warriors.)

My first reaction to hearing about Vicki and her circumstances was unbelief. Brent—my firstborn—and his family were with me as we were walking along a path in Laguna Beach. After the call about Vicki, I felt dizzy and fainted. Luckily Brent caught me before I hit the ground.

It was a very hard thing to imagine and so far out of the ordinary. After a week, I went to Sacramento to visit Mike, Vicki and family. I felt their faith would sustain them through whatever it was they had to face. I prayed constantly for them and when Vicki came home, I went to see what I could do for them. I was amazed at her progress and determination to live her life as fully as she could and share her faith and love for God.

I felt their strength in the acceptance of circumstances and willingness to accept this as what God wanted from them. I see them often and are amazed at their positive attitudes and interests in sharing their story to strengthen others.

Yvonne (Vonnie) Zoradi Davidson (Mike's beloved sister that lives five minutes from our Laguna Niguel home in Southern California. She cleaned our floors each week. Prayer Warrior.)

[Mike's Oldest Brother Steve & Janice]

It's a trick of nature to assume that those who are younger than we will automatically be healthier and easily outlive us. So after sending Vicki a birthday text on July 5, 2018, we weren't unduly concerned when she responded that she needed to pass a kidney stone, and it wasn't exactly how she expected to spend her 60th birthday. Our naiveté kicked in, and we figured it could be a painful, but uneventful birthday at their cabin in Kyburz, California.

Cascading emotions soon enveloped us as we received sketchy details that events were going from bad to worse and then to cataclysmic: Vicki was suddenly and gravely ill, possibly near death. We couldn't sleep, we prayed without ceasing, and we felt utterly helpless. As the days blurred together, Tiffani texted us and said it might be important that we come to Sacramento, as Vicki wasn't expected to live much longer.

Joining the Patterson-Zoradi family in the ICU waiting room meant that we could be part of the prayer team that was right next door to where Vicki was fighting for her life. It gave us confidence to be with the Pattersons, as we all shared the same goal: that God would intercede with a miracle. Our son Ryan soon arrived, and we began the days of waiting, praying, eating hospital food, and holding vigil that Vicki's life could be saved.

God answered our prayers. The hospital staff were astounded, we were rejoicing, and Vicki's natural grit and perseverance joined with God's merciful hand. We were granted our miracle. We will never cease to be thankful beyond measure that the Holy Spirit invaded time and space to spare Vicki's life.

In the weeks that followed, Vicki began her journey of recovery with many medical complications. But she and Mike never gave up hope, and if they could be hopeful, how could any of us be any different? We took our cues from them.

At the end of July, Janice traveled to Jordan with a small team of Christians from Ohio to minister to Syrian refugees who had recently fled their war-torn country. On the day that Vicki's hands and feet were amputated, this stalwart group, strangers to Janice until only a few days prior, prayed together for a woman they had never met in California who was undergoing major surgery. Their empathy, kindness, and strong faith powered those prayers and brought comfort and solidarity. It was truly the body of Christ in action at the other side of the globe.

We all have a purpose in life, and too many never pursue it. Vicki is joy-filled and an amazing example of endurance through adversity. Her life proclaims the eternal truth that God not only answers prayer, but He is good and His mercies are everlasting. She and Mike may be our younger siblings, but they show us the way.

We love you,

Janice and Steve Zoradi (Our much loved brother & sister-in-law from San Luis Obispo, CA., Prayer Warriors)

Receiving Mike's late night text message that Vicki was fighting for her life and in critical condition was so shocking and upsetting. What had started as a kidney stone had so quickly and unexpectedly developed into a very dire situation. We prayed fervently that God would heal her both physically and emotionally and bring her through the crisis. The next weeks and months revealed God's healing hand on Vicki and her endurance of many advances and set-backs. Particularly poignant was being at the hospital the day of her surgical amputations. Vicki's calmness, her faith and her unbelievably positive attitude all comforted her friends and family that were there to support her. She was the one reassuring us that God was in control and that He had a wonderful plan for her life and ministry. Vicki exuded the "peace of God that surpasses all understanding" and she encouraged all of us to rest in God's peace and comfort.

Mark and Cathy Zoradi (Our much loved brother & sister-in-law from Burbank & Santa Barbara, CA., Prayer Warriors, Mobility Comrades)

Aunt Vicki's Story: My Perspective [Niece Noelle]:

I had just arrived in Sacramento airport and was waiting for my baggage with my parents when my mom got an update from the hospital. Aunt Vicki was on life support for three failing organs and needed to be transported to another hospital for any chance of survival. My mom broke down immediately right there in front of the conveyor belt. I think the gravity of losing her sister had finally hit her. She had been in denial, or maybe just highly optimistic up to that point, and even told me I didn't need to fly out. The other members of my family who I talked to on the phone thought otherwise. "I just want you to be here if she passes," my cousin Tiffani told me. "It's very serious... it doesn't look good right now."

We loaded the car and drove straight away to Placerville hospital, where Aunt Vicki was being cared for in ICU. To me, it felt like a race against time. I wanted to arrive at the hospital for a chance to see her before she was taken. I remember my Dad stopped to grab sandwiches on the drive since we had over an hour ahead of us, but I couldn't eat. I had a sick feeling in my gut that left me with no appetite, a feeling that lingered all week. I was in a constant state of nervousness—belly flip flops and shaky limbs—over the possibility that I could lose the woman who had been a second mother to me.

When we arrived at the Placerville hospital, they were not admitting visitors. Aunt Vicki was being prepared for transport by ambulance, a highly risky and life-threatening maneuver. Any small movement in her comatose body sent her vitals through the roof. "How are they expecting her to make it through an ambulance ride?" I thought. I was angry. I was angry at myself that I didn't come sooner. I was angry that I had flown all the way there only to miss her by minutes. I was angry that my dad stopped for sandwiches. There would be no goodbyes, no I love you's or final hugs. The doctors were clear: this ambulance ride to Sacramento hospital would be the only way to save her life, but it was not likely that she would make it through the ride. I watched the ambulance drive away with Aunt Vicki and with my hope.

The only thing to do was get back in the car and return to Sacramento, to the hospital where she was being transported. I braced myself the entire ride for the phone call I anticipated. The phone call which would notify us of Aunt Vicki's passing. Minute by minute passed, but somehow we arrived at Sacramento hospital without any news. My body felt the urge to RUN into the hospital as soon as I stepped foot in the parking lot, as if that would change any outcomes. Every step I was nervous and shaky, because, in my gut, I felt God was preparing me for news of Aunt Vicki's death.

After what felt like the longest walk of my life, our family greeted us in the waiting room with hesitant smiles that she survived the ambulance ride. Though Aunt Vicki was still alive, the doctors prepared the family that this would be a roller coaster ride. They did not project any hope for her recovery. We gathered in a circle, with our arms around each other and prayed fervently, as we would do constantly over the next seven days.

There was a private waiting room in the ICU which our family quickly occupied. It was the perfect set up for us, a subtle yet undeniable gift from God. The room had a door that closed allowing us the privacy to come together to pray, to cry, to sleep, to eat, or not eat. There was a long, padded window seat, a couple reclining chairs, and a handful of regular chairs, accommodating the whole family. The outside window overlooked the city of Sacramento and the inside window alerted us to doctors comings and goings. Aside from all these perks, the best part about the space was that it shared a wall with aunt Vicki's ICU room. I hoped she could feel our prayers from the other side of the wall.

When Aunt Vicki was settled in her room and "stable," I was able to see her for the first time. As I entered her room, the first thing I noticed was the plethora of machines surrounding her bed. There was hardly any square foot of free space. There were tubes and wires and monitors and bags of liquid hanging everywhere. Then I saw Aunt Vicki's face. Nothing can really prepare you to see a family member in this condition. It was as if she was gone already. Her once beautiful and kind eyes bulged out of their sockets, so red and bloodshot that I could hardly find the white of her eyes. Her head cocked to one side and a ventilator in her throat mechanically moved her head forward and backward. She had stringy hair plastered back from her face as if she was wind-blown. The combination made her look wild and petrified. Her skin was discolored and her body was puffy from being filled with fluids. She laid lifeless with her giant, crimson eyes that stared blankly. People will tell you that life support patients can hear you, so you should talk to them. I knew she couldn't hear me, but I talked to her anyway. I put on my brave voice and told her I was there and that I loved her. I made awkward one-way conversation about my toddler and my plane ride until I could no longer maintain my composure. I left her room and cried. I understood in that moment how grave her condition was. I questioned if it was cruel to continue keeping her alive because it looked like she was suffering. The pain of seeing her this way was unbearable, and I just wanted her to be at peace.

Hours passed and Aunt Vicki's condition seemed to worsen. Medical jargon, information about intervention, waivers for experimental drugs and conversations about her vitals and statistics filled most of the airtime. At any given moment, three nurses worked around the clock in her room giving medication, fluids or adjusting the tubes and machinery which kept her alive. Every time the doctors would come in to update us, we would respond by joining together and praying over what the doctors said she needed. These prayer circles were the most profound symbol of strength and unity in Christ that I have ever witnessed. We prayed vigorously, quoting scripture and singing praises. We begged God to save her life. It was physically uncomfortable for me to wrap my arms around my family during our prayer circles because of the snot running down my nose each time we prayed. As the updates worsened, the fervency increased. We cried, we sobbed, we held each other, and we prayed more. At one point, Uncle Mike cried out to God, his voice cracking through tears and anguish and said, "If you take Vicki, I will still love you and serve you, God. You are sovereign." The gravity of that statement hit me in the gut, and I sobbed. In his weakest hour, my uncle proclaimed his faith more strongly with those words than he ever could have before. He had fully submitted to God's will, an unfathomable expression of devotion in that moment.

Family members blasted group texts out to the church community, pastors, friends and family calling for prayer. There were so many people praying with us and supporting us. While we prayed and gathered as a family, we alternated who was physically present with Aunt Vicki so she could also hear scripture and hymns. The physical and emotional weight of the circumstance was so heavy that we literally couldn't cry or pray any more. It was growing late into the night and we knew we couldn't all sleep in the waiting room. Eventually, we went home to my parents' house. That night, I got on my knees in the dark bedroom and sobbed. I begged God to change his mind. It was clear to me that Aunt Vicki was dying, and even though I knew He had a plan for this, I asked him for a miracle that would bring even more glory to Him.

The next morning was more of the same emotional roller coaster. Aunt Vicki's body began to balloon from all the fluids and medications. Her fingers and toes began to turn purple as the blood was pulled from them to keep her heart pumping. Even the tip of her nose had turned purple, which made her look even more like a corpse. It could have been anyone laying in that hospital bed because she was so unrecognizable. She had an air blanket laid all around her that resembled a pool float so that only her face was showing. The nurses could no longer get a blood pressure reading because her body was so enlarged. None of the experimental drugs or sepsis protocols were working. Her body was simply failing. The doctors sent for the hospital chaplain to provide comfort to our family. The chaplain's presence was confirmation to me of what I had felt in my gut all along, that Aunt Vicki would die.

We gathered around her bedside to say our final goodbyes. We sang hymns such as "Great is Thy Faithfulness," in unison, the ten voices filling the room. My Uncle Mike sat behind her, lovingly stroking her hair, kissing her face and telling her how much he loved and adored her. "No one will ever replace you, Vic," he cried. It was an emotional catharsis as each person shared out how much she meant to them. The goodbyes continued until there were no more words to give. I thought again about how it seemed cruel to keep her alive in this condition and wondered how much she was suffering. I didn't want this to be the last image in my mind of my aunt. I glanced from time to time to the heart monitor, waiting for the final moment and for peace, but the thin neon line continued to make small peaks on the screen. The waiting was painful. We had said our goodbyes, prayed our final prayers and submitted her to the Lord's will. I couldn't understand why she continued to suffer. I longed for finality so I didn't have to continue to witness the agony. Eventually night came, and not knowing what else to do, we returned home to await the call of her passing.

I called my husband that night, crying and telling him all that had happened. I couldn't sleep, but was so desperately exhausted. My body and my soul were drained. I wasn't ready to face the news the morning would bring and somehow thought that delaying sleep could prevent it.

After a restless night, I woke up in the morning to the sounds of lively chatter. I suddenly remembered the circumstance and thought it was odd to hear this kind of liveliness. I heard my parents and aunt and uncle making breakfast and talking joyfully. I knew then, something was different. I promptly got out of bed to see what had happened.

"Did you hear?" my mom exclaimed, "It's a miracle!" when I emerged from my bedroom puffy eyed. "Aunt Vicki turned a corner!" I couldn't believe my ears and wondered if I was dreaming. My family filled me in with her statistics and her improvements while I stood, stunned. Apparently, that night, aunt Vicki's body miraculously began to stabilize without any rational explanation. A flood of relief washed over me. I returned to my bedroom and cried tears of relief, thanking God for listening to our prayers and saving Aunt Vicki's life. For the first time in days, my appetite returned.

It started sinking in that this was a true miracle that I witnessed and I still couldn't wrap my head around it. It didn't make any sense medically or scientifically. I remembered the chaplain, I remembered our goodbyes, I remembered Aunt Vicki's blood pressure that wasn't capable of sustaining life and I remember Aunt Vicki's unrecognizable body. I knew beyond a shadow of a doubt that God heard our prayers and intervened. He chose to save my Aunt Vicki's life and he would use her life to bring glory to Him, just as we had prayed. I felt in my soul that God changed his mind.

The coming days were filled with trials and challenges, but each day there was gradual progress. By the time I left, my Aunt Vicki had been able to blink three time for "I love you," a comfort to my soul. I left Sacramento with a renewed sense of faith and awe of God's power and love for us. I saw God breathe life into Aunt Vicki's ravaged body, in a way that no other medical intervention was able to.

After coming home, I reflected on all that I had seen. Witnessing Aunt Vicki's miracle re-affirmed a few principles in my own faith. First, God is all-powerful and mighty to save. It's easy to forget, living in a western culture, that there is a spiritual realm, all unseen to our eyes. After seeing God's work of saving Aunt Vicki's life, I have no doubt that miracles are not bound to first century, biblical stories. God is still the same God who rescued the Israelites from Egypt, and the same God who rose Jesus from the grave. He remains almighty, and Aunt Vicki's healing is an example of this. Second, prayer is powerful. God truly listened to the prayers of hundreds, if not thousands, of people who were praying. I serve a God who is not only omnipotent, but loves us and hears us when we talk to him. Third, there is immeasurable value in the Christian community. The support pouring out from the church was overwhelming. Hundreds of Christians were praying for Aunt Vicki, dozens sent care packages and other forms of tangible support, handfuls offered their homes for accommodations, and many visited in person to pray over Aunt Vicki directly. I witnessed firsthand the church community living out what it means to love and support one another through trials. This is the type of community that I want surrounding me.

With my faith renewed, I looked to the future with anticipation of how God would use Aunt Vicki's story. I witnessed God's power, the effectiveness of prayer, and a community of believers coming together. But Aunt Vicki's journey had only just begun to unfold and she would have much more story to tell.

Love,

Noelle Parks Kaiser (Niece, Sister Valori's and Brother-in Law Paul's daughter who resides with her husband Steven and their son, Harrison, in Seattle, WA., Exemplary Teacher, Prayer Warrior)

Vicki Darling,

When I was called and told that my niece was in critical shape with sepsis and dying, I rushed up to Sacramento to be with her and the family. The night before, her doctors told her husband, Mike, that Vicki wouldn't make it through the night. When I arrived in the morning, I was greeted by Mike and Vicki's brother-in-law, Paul, who was out in the hall. With tears & joy, they were praising the Lord that God had spared Vicki's life. Vicki continued to be on total life support. Vicki's journey to wellness has been a very long journey with her putting her total trust in God. When she was told much later by her husband that she would have to have her arms and legs amputated, she told him, "Well, I will have a ministry then." The night before her surgery, she prayed for God to heal her so she wouldn't have to go through the surgery. But...God said, "NO, I WILL BE YOUR HANDS AND FEET." And now, as I write this, Vicki just told me that, "If only one life came to faith in Christ, it would be worth all my pain and loss."

Aunt Peggy Forbes Kind (Vicki's mother's younger sister who resides in Petaluma, CA., Prayer Warrior)

[Friends John & Debbie Helfrich]

We have been friends with Vicki and Mike for over 30 years and have always been inspired by their faith in the Lord and their loving marriage. Two years ago their faith was tested.

We got a phone call from Mike in the middle of the night telling us that Vicki was fighting for her life and asking us to pray for her. We were shocked and devastated and began praying for God to heal our dear friend. She was on our minds all the time especially when we would be at their house to feed their cat. While we were there, we noticed a calendar that hung in the garage. It had all kinds of upcoming events penciled in but they were now in a hospital just praying she would survive.

It made us think about how our lives are in God's hands. We never know what the future holds and we should thank God daily for all he has given us. It didn't seem real that she was in a life and death battle up north and we couldn't even be there to support Mike. He would text updates asking for prayer for specific health concerns. Throughout her battle, as her organs were shutting down and her blood pressure would start dropping, Mike just trusted the Lord and put Vicki's life in His hands.

Vicki's story strengthened our firm belief in the power of prayer and that God brings good out of terrible circumstances. By all medical accounts, Vicki should not be alive. There was no other explanation than a miracle from God. Vicki and Mike both know that Jesus wanted to use her life to bring others to know Him. During that time especially and still now, we look at Vicki and are amazed at how she has handled a life changing loss of all her limbs without complaining. Mike has been her loving partner, caregiver and encourager throughout and Vicki has a calmness and peace that would be impossible without her strong faith and love for Jesus. We thank God that we have our precious friend with us today.

John & Debbie Helfrich (Best friends for over 30 years, Met at Grace Community Church, Racquetball, Pickle-ball, Baseball, Co-Ed Softball Team, Card Partners, Prayer Warriors)

[Friends Russ & Dottie Eastman]

We got a call from our friends, John and Debbie Helfrich, on July 8, 2018 letting us know that Vicki had been taken to the ER up by their cabin on her birthday July 5th. Mike had suspected it was her appendix. It turned out to be kidney stones. She was now back in the hospital and not doing well. Russ and I immediately started praying for her and Mike. Our hearts were hurting for our dear friends as they faced what seemed like an insurmountable situation. We knew that our God was bigger than this situation so we petitioned Him for a miracle. By God's grace and mercy, He heard our prayers and those of many others. Over the course of the next several months, Mike sent out many prayer requests via text as Vicki's organs began shutting down one by one. Each time, God heard the cry of His people as we petitioned Him on Vicki's behalf. We are so blessed to have our Miracle Girl with us. Her testimony has touched many lives including ours.

Love You,

Russ & Dottie Eastman (Original Church Friends from Mission Viejo since 1987, Baseball, Racquetball, Pickle-ball, Co-Ed Softball Team, Card Partners, Prayer Warriors)

[Mark–HFG Leader]

Ephesians 3:20-21—"Now to him who is able to do far more abundantly than all we ask or think, according to the power at work within us, to him be glory in the church and in Christ Jesus throughout all generations, forever and ever. Amen."

Vicki- I am so amazed at the courage and joy that you and Mike displayed in this unimaginable journey these past 2 years. Jeanette and I were in Palm Springs and just went through changing rooms at 1:00 in the morning which is the only reason we were awake when Mike called me. All he said through hard tears was, "I am losing the love of my life!" Immediately, we hit our knees and began praying for you and Mike. This started us down a journey of talking to Mike every day and getting specific in our prayers and communicating with so many others to specifically pray for your hourly needs. We saw God come through so many times with "razor thin" timing when the experts were giving up on you. There were many times when seeing Mike calling me, I could not help thinking, 'Is this the call telling me the struggle is over?' only to learn that God had answered a specific prayer miraculously. Jeanette and I have felt honored to be part of the inner circle of your family and love and cherish our friendship so much. You and Mike have taught us what it really means to involve the community of believers in your need for prayer and to trust God completely for the final results. You have and will continue to touch so many lives for Christ as you tell your amazing story of faith, prayer and perseverance.

Mark O'Connor (Home Fellowship Leader, Friend, Inner Circle, Prayer Warrior)

[Jeanette HFG-Co-Leader]

231

A call from Mike came in asking for prayer for his precious Vicki. God had already orchestrated HIS Sovereignty by having us already awake at 2:30am in the morning. A moment that orchestrated many future calls, texts and emails asking for others to pray. This became the beginning of a great and powerful prayer train. Prayer Warriors who loved them both so deeply and cried out to their faithful and powerful GOD mightily, often throughout each day for many months. What a privilege to have had witnessed the fingerprints of God working each day.

When I reflect back on that season, three memories come to my heart that touched me deeply. The Sovereignty and timing of God despite what Man does, the humility of my friends, despite what occurred and a bold and loving example of a Christian marriage that so desired to honor God and give HIM all the Glory.

"In the same way, let your light shine before others, so that they may see your good works and give glory to your Father who is in heaven." Matthew 5:16

Love,

Jeanette O'Connor (Home Fellowship Group Co-Leader, Women's Bible Study Group, Friend, Inner Circle, Prayer Warrior)

[Alisa's Memories]

Vicki and I started teaching within a year of each other. We quickly became not only colleagues, but close friends. Several years later, we became teaching partners, sharing a class between the two of us. This was a blessing for us both, as we were able to spend more time with our families on the days we didn't teach. We did this off and on over many years.

Like dozens of summers before, I texted Vicki on her birthday. I knew she was up at the cabin with her family, so when I didn't hear back from her, I figured she was enjoying time with them. A few days and several

232

unanswered texts went by and Tammy, a fellow teacher from Lake Forest Elementary School, texted me and asked me what was wrong with Vicki. I responded that I didn't know and that I had texted several times, with no response. She said that she had gotten a text from Mike asking for prayers for Vicki.

I reached out to my family and friends, who all started praying for her. We didn't know the extent of the need for the prayers at the time, but we knew Vicki and her family needed divine intervention. Over the course of the next few days, the details of her illness began to be shared. There was a text chain started at our school. As details came from Mike and Tiffani, we would share them with our staff. Prayers from teachers of all faiths began to go up on behalf of Vicki. Prior to this experience, our staff was not big on sharing their religious beliefs. Most of us knew who was Christian, Catholic, Jewish, atheist, etc. A few strong Christian women had started a 'before school' prayer group, but it wasn't until Vicki's experience that we truly opened up our hearts and prayed as one, regardless of faith, as children of a loving Heavenly Father who was truly able to hear our pleadings and bestow healing on our dear friend in her time of need.

After weeks of recovery in Northern California, Tammy and I went to visit Vicki in a hospital she had been transferred to in Orange County, closer to home. We walked into her room and were shocked to see our beautiful Vicki laying in a hospital bed with her hands and feet bandaged. Her manicured fingers and toenails a stark contrast against her blackened, dying skin. Both Mike & Vicki shared the heartbreaking and unbelievably incredible story she is sharing in this book with us. At that time, doctors were still trying to save her hands and feet, but as Vicki shares, that miracle was not to be. Our prayers for complete healing and recovering the use of her hands and feet would not be answered.

Instead, she was to begin a new chapter in her life, a chapter where her story of faith would touch millions of people, a chapter that might not have happened if God had listened to our pleadings for complete recovery and healing. Weeks later, as a new school year was to begin, I shared with the staff the news that Vicki would be having surgery to remove her hands and feet. There was not a dry eye in the room. Our staff sat stunned at the news. People could not believe that our once vivacious friend and colleague was having to endure this trial of faith.

233

As Vicki shares, her journey was one of struggle and recovery and as her body healed, her desire to share God's amazing grace with others increased. This past school year, Vicki was able to once again walk through the halls of our school. On her new feet, she came into the classroom, a room we had once shared together, and talked with my students, who sat in awe of the 'Robot Teacher', as Vicki shared a real life STEAM lesson with my class, showing them how her prosthetic fingers, hands and legs worked. Afterward, she was able to reconnect with several former students and families, many who had been praying for her as well.

And so, Vicki continues to teach as she shares her incredible message of her experience and how God has been able to use her as a tool to reach others and share his message of love, hope and unanswered prayers. HIS plan is divine.

Alisa Bowen (SVUSD Teacher, Colleague, Teaching Partner, Friday Lunch Buddy, Friend, Teacher Prayer Chain VP)

My Dear Sweet Vicki, [Tammy—Teacher]

Learning about your sepsis through your daughter, Tiffani's Facebook page threw me into action mode, with a series of events that would end up changing lives for Jesus through the "foxhole" God was asking you to endure. Here's Your journey, V, through my eyes....

Tiffani called after I contacted her on Facebook and was in tears telling me how serious your condition was. It took me a moment to process what your precious child was actually telling me. My ears heard, but my brain just couldn't or possibly wouldn't allow any sense of comprehension filter. My friend may be going home to Jesus! In that moment I told Tiffani to put the phone on speaker and take the phone over to your ear. With Tiffani crying in the background, I rattled off a prayer for the power of Jesus to do what the doctors couldn't. I don't remember any of the words, but I did feel Jesus.

Tiffani gave me Mike's number and he graciously and patiently (he called me the persistent widow from the bible) began to correspond with me about the details. I reached out to as many prayer chains as I could down in Southern California because...you were dying Vicki. It was a long night of your family lifting you up in prayer in Sacramento while an army of believers were equally petitioning God for a miracle here in the Southland.

The next morning I read Mike's text and began crying, "No Lord why did you take her? Didn't you hear the prayers?" My husband asked what was going on and I told him you went home to Jesus. Fast forward literally 3 minutes later...I reread Mike's text and wiping tears and snot from my face I saw it clearly. God hadn't taken you, He breathed life into you at the "end" of the 11th hour. I only saw the word "end" the first time. Hallelujahs and praises were being shouted by the prayer warriors down South.

Since you were a teacher, many of the staff had now heard about your near death experience and were hungry for any news they could get. What started off with about five Christian teachers texting each other with messages that I would forward from Mike ended up being a mission field for the unsaved teachers who asked to join. For days I got requests from staff, past and present, who asked to be added to the feed with the final count totaling somewhere around 28. Your story and Jesus' miracle was so riveting, that they couldn't get enough. I almost had to beg Mike for info if a day or two went by without a word.

It's now obvious when I think back on that feed, that God started writing your story waaaaay back in the beginning of your journey because your "foxhole" was going to reach the hearts of those who needed to either have their faith strengthened through this miracle, or be part of a journey that was real, unscripted, and clearly controlled by the hand of God. Thank you Mike for putting up with this persistent lady!

I called the site LFE Miracle and made no apologies for the bold Christian content that would be the central focus of the feed. I must say I was a bit nervous sending Jesus to a bunch of unsaved "public" school teachers, but God used that site to show His love and power through your story. I began saving the feeds for you and sending a few copies each day so you could read for yourself what people were saying.

235

Coming to visit you at the rehab center once you arrived in Orange County made your miracle that much more precious to me. You didn't hesitate to show me your dead feet and hands. They were black and puffy and clearly beyond life. They reminded me of what a mummy's uncovered body might look like, but for some odd reason I wasn't grossed out or afraid at all. Quite the opposite. I held your hand and started massaging it. I have no idea why and looking back now it was a silly gesture. Dummy me! Perhaps it was the purple polish on your nails which was so you. Ha-ha.

God took this "foxhole" you and Mike were in and brought forth a platform to spread the Gospel far and wide. You wasted no time answering the call and began speaking to groups on how Jesus, the Son of God, came down to touch you with a modern day miracle so His name could be glorified. To God be the Glory forever and ever. Amen

Love you Friend,

Tammy Strand (SVUSD Teacher/Colleague/Friend/Prayer Chain President, Prayer Warrior)

—————————————

My Thoughts...[Bonnie—Teacher]

The crushing email news I read from former teaching colleagues left me stunned and heartbroken. I was grasping for some understanding from our good God of what He had allowed to happen to my vibrant and healthy friend Vicki and His cherished daughter.

I learned she was not at their family cabin, but in an induced coma in a desperate attempt to save her life. Vicki's condition was too unbelievable for me to comprehend and there was only one thing I could do that mattered. That was to cry out to our merciful and mighty God for His healing miracles that were far beyond what any doctor could do.

Throughout the coming days, I cried out to God in prayer continually while hearing more devastating news of her failing condition and the imminent threat of losing her hands and feet. I held on to God's promises for help, knowing He is able to do all things and full of compassion, as many prayers were lifted up by family and friends. God surely rescued her from death but answered prayers to save her hands and feet in a way I did not pray for or could understand.

Nearly two years have passed as I write this since Vicki's hospitalization and subsequent amputations. Now, I have more clearly seen God's unfolding, glorious plan through many miracles of healing for all to see. His loving hands have tenderly molded my treasured friend into a beautiful, radiant and powerful testimony of His loving kindness, faithfulness and power.

I have witnessed Vicki becoming His hands and feet in a new way to share the message of His saving love through Jesus Christ. He has become her hands and feet, all for His glory. For this I am in awe of His love and greatness above all things to bring such beauty out of ashes.

"Trust in him at all times, O people; pour out your heart before Him; God is a refuge for us." Psalm 62:8

Bonnie Osborne (Former Teaching Colleague, Forever Friend, Lunch Buddy, Prayer Warrior)

—————————————

Hello Vicki! [Friend Donna Sellers]

So grateful that you continue to serve GOD in ways HE knew but we all did not.

I found out about your circumstances the night you first went to the hospital in Sacramento area from Jeanette as a prayer request. Thinking you would be treated, maybe spend a day in the hospital and be fine. Did not see the months of hospital stays that were ahead of you And the life change that would come. GOD knew. GOD has your loving husband by your side updating prayer requests daily/as needed so the army of people praying for you could continue to lift you up. There were tears of sadness when things looked bleak. There were tears of joy when GOD said 'she is my child and she has more to do for me' and your body rebounded. GOD, you and Mike have shown what trust in GOD and a family is when difficult circumstances occur. GOD is always present 'HE never leaves us nor forsakes us.' Isaiah 41:10 was prayed for you often.

It has been a privilege and joy to pray for you then and continue to pray as you make an eternal impact for HIS Kingdom. I have a big heart for prayer as my time with GOD. Think of how we prayed over every detail not even knowing at times if HE would have you still here with us. Although we prayed hard that HE would allow you to keep your hands and feet, HE chose differently. Look at how GOD is having you reach SO many people with your story. Always makes me think of being the 'hands and feet of JESUS' which you are!

Donna Sellers (New Friend since 2019, Quilting Buddy, Prayer Warrior)

I [Rick Myers] first heard about Vicki's sepsis through a church prayer line. While so often fatal, my clinical practice is often needed to provide prosthetics for sepsis patients, as many lose limbs. Next was a text from one of the Pastors with Mike's phone number. A couple of messages and phone conversations later, I was standing with Mike and Vicki at Long Beach Memorial. Over the next year, I have been blessed to work with Mike, Vicki, and Tiffani as Vicki has fought and struggled and progressed to relearn life and train for her new ministry! It is an incredible blessing to now see Mike and Vicki enter this new chapter of their life serving Christ, newly equipped for good work!

Kind Regards,

Rick Myers, Owner CEO, Southern California Prosthetics (Caring Friend, Spiritual Brother, Mobility Expert)

I first met Vicki in September of 2018. I am the Office Manager at her prosthetic facility. I remember hearing about her limb loss and feeling so sad for her. I expected her to come in discouraged as many new amputees do. Losing just one limb will radically shake one's life. Losing 2 or 3 limbs is a massive loss. But the impact of losing all four limbs is inconceivable! In light of this, Vicki surprised me from day one. She came in smiling. She actually radiated true joy. It was clear that she wasn't faking it. Appointment after appointment after appointment, even when it was extremely painful and difficult, she always smiled and she literally never complained. I knew she was the real deal and that she knew her God! I have so many memories of Vicki laughing as she learned to use a fork (her wrists on her prosthetic hands were making full 360 degree turns as she learned to control them). I remember laughing so hard with her as I filmed her trying to throw the frisbee for the office dogs! She would fling her wrist but then her hand wouldn't release the frisbee until later and the frisbee would fall to the ground. She honestly could've cried, but she laughed!! We all laughed because her joy is contagious. Her hubby, Mike, has been amazing in this whole process. He has been at her side always cheering her on (literally)!! I am honored to be a part of their amazing journey and excited to see what Jesus has in mind as they daily surrender joyfully to His plan!

Kind Regards,

Teresa Crabbe, Office Manager, Southern California Prosthetics (A Sweet Friend, Spiritual Sister, One who is willing to go the extra mile)

Vicki - [Mary—My Amazing School Volunteer]

When I first heard through Tammy Klein and Alisa Bowen from Lake Forest Elementary School, I was scared for you and your family! I knew that you were always with family and friends who had so much faith, but it seemed almost overwhelming that your health was so bad. I sometimes wondered if faith could pull you through. I guess I questioned my faith, too, as this seemed so monumental!!

When told that you had survived all issues including losing your limbs, I knew that your faith was much stronger than all could even imagine. I also knew that if anyone could possibly go through the pain, hard work and the mental part of this, it would definitely be you and Mike!!

Seeing your patience with second-graders and especially their parents and constant changing of command and rules at school, I figure you would give it the best shot that you could and that you would leave it all in God's hands! I have learned a lot from you especially in keeping the faith and power of prayer.

The prayers that you shared with me and for praying for Taylor, (my grandchild and your former student, who is on the mend at home adjusting to her new doctors and medicines), showed me again at my age the complete power of prayer and putting all things into God's hands—working with Him along side of you helping you to succeed in health, relationships, family and life in general!

Much love, hugs n kisses,

Grandma Mary Q. (Super Volunteer for each employee at LFE for many, many years! Could not have taught as effectively without her countless hours in our workroom at school.)

[Pattie] One of the most encouraging verses in the Bible is Romans 8:28. This verse helps the Christian to think of things differently than the non-believer. God is the giver of only good gifts to those who are his. This promise from the Word of God to the true Christian is, "And we know that for those who love God all things work together for good, for those who are called according to his purpose." Vicki Zoradi is one of the obvious recipients of God's blessings by his working all things together for good in her life. As a recent quadruple amputee, Vicki has been given a ministry to share all the good that God has done through her life, illness, and recovery. She is never without a smile on her face and the joy of the Lord is ever radiating from her life. To know her is to love her! I hope by reading this book it blessed your life and gave you a boost of encouragement!!!

Pattie Brown (Women's Bible Study, Friend, Sunset photographer, Encourager)

Vicki Zoradi,

I watched your story online while we were at Paul and Val's last week (Paul and Bill are cousins). What an AMAZING healing you experienced! As a retired RN, I recognize how miraculous your survival is. Thank you for sharing your story. May our Lord continue to heal and bless you and your family.

Linda Greene (RN, FB friend message)

I worked at Medcom for 45 years. Many, many with Mike. I have survived cancer 2xs. But Vicki, you are so such an inspiration and that is above & beyond. Prayers always. Love to be in your uplifting progress. I would love to purchase your book when it's released.

Hugs always,

Diane Cascarelli (Mike's former co-worker, FB friend message)

Throughout my entire pilgrimage, I knew I was loved and loved very well. I thoroughly enjoyed these words of love that I never heard on July 9th, 2018. My God, my family, and my friends were quite evident during all of my trials. When *tested by fire,* it is much more tolerable when fully *fueled by faith.* May God bless us all until we finish our eventful FINAL RACE here on earth as we cross the finish line and see...

The Checkered Flag Waves.

"RACE TO WIN!"

BUT GOD...

"But I trust in you, O LORD; I say, 'You are my God.'" Psalm 31:14

"Let love be genuine. Abhor what is evil; hold fast to what is good. Love one another with brotherly affection. Outdo one another in showing honor. Do not be slothful in zeal, be fervent in spirit, serve the Lord. Rejoice in hope, be patient in tribulation, be constant in prayer." Romans 12:9-12

Check out videos, pod-casts, additional photos, and
"The Vicki Zoradi Story" at: vickizoradi.com

@vickizoradi #vickizoradi
@Quad4God #Quad4God

Follow Vicki on Facebook, Instagram, and Twitter

vickizoradi@gmail.com

S-T-E-A-M Lesson—"Robotics!"

BIBLIOGRAPHY

Title: Tested by Fire...Fueled by Faith. Flier. Both used with permission. Dara Linson, JWP. [ChibadofMV.com.]

Prologue

[1] *"Racing Flags."* 2008, January. WIKIPEDIA. 09/08/2020. [en.m.wikipedia.org].

Chapter 1   Perplexing Predicament

[1] Kochoff, Anya: Writer. Luketic, Robert: Director. Bender, Chris. Spink, J.C. Weinstein, Paula: Producers. 2005/05/05. *"Monster-in-Law."* Spring Creek Pictures. 09/06/2020. [en.m.wikipedia].

[2] Mayo Clinic Staff. 2018. *Overview, Symptoms, Causes, Risk Factors and Complications of Sepsis and Septic Shock.* Mayo Clinic Family Health. Book. 5th Edition. 06/13/20. [mayoclinic.org]

[3] O'Connell, Krista. August 31, 2018. *Sepsis.* 08/30/20. [healthline.com]

[4] *"NASCAR rules and regulations. SubTitle: Car and driver changes."* 2013, July. NASCAR. National Association for Stock Car Auto Racing. WIKIPEDIA. 09/08/2020. [en.m.wikipedia.org].

Chapter 2   Power of Prayer

[1] weathergirl15. 2014. *And, They Told Two Friends, and So On and So On.* Results Communications and Research - Marketing and Market Research Services. 08/30/20. [allintheresults.com]

[2] Compass Bible Church * 140 Columbia, Aliso Viejo, California 92656 * Pastor: Mike Fabarez

[3] *Used With Permission* from each e-mail author. Home Fellowship Group (HFG). **Compass Bible Church**. Aliso Viejo, California.

[4] Roseveare, Helen. 2011. *"Suffering for Jesus is a privilege," says veteran missionary.* Christian Today Article (Author not sited). 08/30/20. [christiantoday.com] Quote from missionary Helen Roseveare.

[5] Zemeckis, Robert and Gale, Bob: Writers. Zemeckis, Robert: Director. Gale, Bob and Canton, Neil: Producers. 7/3/1985. *"Back to the Future."* Universal Pictures; Amblin Entertainment. 09/06/2020. [en.m.wikipedia.org].

Chapter 3   Providential Plans & Purposes

[1] Author Unknown. "The Game of Life History - Invention of the Game of Life." 2006. *The Great Idea Finder.* Archived from the original. 09/11/2019. [en.m.wikipedia.org].

[2] Lamm, Robert: Writer. Guerico, James William: Producer. Recorded 1971/09. *"Saturday in the Park,"* Chicago V. 1972. 09/07/2020. [en.m.wikipedia.org].

[3] McCartney, Paul. Lennon-McCartney partnership. 1968. *"Let It Be,"* The Beatles (White Album / Super Deluxe) Single Released: 1970/03/06. 09/07/2020 [en.m.wikipedia.org].

[4] Gunther, William and Iva. 1948/08. *"About Gunther's,"* GUNTHER'S ICE CREAM, 09/07/2020. [gunthersicecream.com].

[5] Knudson, Jim and Margaret. 1954. *"Jimboy's Tacos,"* Sacramento Headquarters. 09/07/2020. [en.m.wikipedia.org].

[6] Medcom, Inc. 1987. *"For Over 50 Years,"* MEDCOM. 09/07/2020. [medcominc.com].

Chapter 4   Peace, Sweet Peace

[1] Bibendum. French. 1894. "Michelin Man." Michelin Tyre Company. WIKIPEDIA. 09/11/2020. [en.m.wikipedia.org].

[2] Knievel, Robert Craig. October 17, 1938-November 30, 2007. *"Evel Knievel."* Stunt Performer. evelknievel.com. WIKIPEDIA. 09/11/2020. [en.m.wikipedia.org].

[3] Hunting, Benjamin. 2009. "50 Years of Barbie's Rides." autobytel. 09/11/2020. [autobytel.com].

[4] Stallone, Sylvester: Writer, Director, Actor. 2006. *"Rocky Balboa (film)."* Sequel #6 of Rocky V. 1990. Rocky Film Series. WIKIPEDIA. 09/12/2020. [en.m.wikipedia.com].

[5] Butterworth, Jez and John Henry; Keller, Jason: Writers. Chernin, Peter; Topping, Jenno; Mangold, James: Producers. Chernin Entertainment; TSG Entertainment: Production Companies. 2019. *"Ford v Ferrari."* WIKIPEDIA. 09/10/2020. [en.m.wikipedia.org].

[6] Lasseter, John; Ranft, Joe; Klubien, Jorge: Writers. 2006/May 26. *"Cars (film)." Walt Disney Pictures; Pixar Animation Studio: Production Companies. Anderson, Darla K: Producer. WIKIPEDIA. 09/16/2020.* [moviecars2006.google.com; en.m.wikipedia.com].

[7] CCLI Song # 27714—Charles Crozat Converse | Joseph Medlicott Scrivener—Copyrighted Words: Public Domain—For use solely with the SongSelect. All rights reserved.—songselect.ccli.com—What A Friend We Have In Jesus—Public Domain—(1855).

Chapter 5   Pushing Through Pain...

[1] Hei Hei, Rabbi Ben. Second Century. "According to the pain is the gain." - (Hebrew) Pirkei Avot 5:23. The Ethics of the Fathers 5:21. No pain, no gain. WIKIPEDIA. 09/13/2020. [en.m.wikipedia.org].

[2] Herrick, Robert. 1650 edition. Hesperides. "NO PAINS, NO GAINS" - Origin. WIKIPEDIA. 09/13/2020. [en.m.wikipedia.org].

[3] Franklin, Benjamin. 1734. Poor Richard. *Axiom: "God helps those who help themselves."* WIKIPEDIA. 09/13/2020. [gen.m.wikipedia.org].

[4] "Septicemia". Subtitle: "What are the symptoms of sepsis?" 2020. JOHNS HOPKINS MEDICINE. 09/14/2020. [httpso://www.hopkinsmedicine.org].

[5] Hanyu-Deutmeyer, AA, Cascella, M, Varacallo, M. Phantom Limb Pain. [Updated 2020 Jul 4]. In: StatPearls [Internet]. Treasure Island (FL): StatPearls Publishing; 2020 Jan-. [ncbi.nlm.nih.gov].

[6] http so://www.emedicinehealth.com

Chapter 6   Prosthetics: Pain, Pitfalls and Pleasures

[1] Cameron, James: Writer, Director. Hurd, Gale Anne: Writer, Producer. 1984/ October 26. *"Terminator."* Hemdale and Pacific Western Productions: Production Companies. Orion Pictures. Starring: Arnold Schwarzenegger. WIKIPEDIA. 09/19/2020. [en.m.wkipedia.com].

[2] Johnson, Kenneth. Based on: Caidin, Martin.*"Cyborg."* 1976. *"The Bionic Woman."* ABC. Universal Television Production. Starring: Lindsay Wagner. 09/19/2020. WIKIPEDIA.[en.m.wikipedia.com].

Chapter 7   Perfect Hope / Pure Joy

[1] Jeremiah, David. 2017/10/03. *"Bible Gateway | Life More Abundant: An Interview with David Jeremiah.* A Life Beyond Amazing: 9 Decisions That Will Transform Your Life Today. (Thomas Nelson, 2017). The KAIROS Company. 08/31/2020. [thekcompany.com].

[2] Jeremiah, David. 2017. *"Top 30 Quotes of DAVID JEREMIAH Famous Quotes."* Inspiring Quotes. 08/31/202.[www.inspiringquotes.us].— [2]Jeremiah, David. 2004. *"Prayer, the Great Adventure."* Goodreads. 08/31/2020. [goodreads.com]

[3] Fabarez, Mike; Pastor. Compass Bible Church. 20*13/10/07. "Quote of the Day ~ Dr. Mike Fabarez on Resolve."* 09/21/2020. [holyjustlove.com].

[4] Wide World of Sports Intro 1974. *The 8th Motive."* ABC. American Broadcasting Company. 10/15/2020. [youtube.com].

[5] Friel, Todd. **Don't Stub Your Toe** - It Could Be The LAST Thing You Ever Do. Alpharetta, Georgia. Gospel Partners Media. 2017.

[6] Fabarez, Mike. Pastor/Author/Speaker. *"What is the Gospel?"* COMPASS BIBLE CHURCH. YouTube. 09/23/2020. [youtube.com].

[7] *"The Person And Work of the Holy Spirit."*(1). 2020/10/15. [moodybible.org].

[8] Eareckson Tada, Joni. Quotes as picture used with permission.

[9] Vujicic, Nick. 2007/08/31. *"Life Without Limits: Inspiration for a Ridiculously Good Life."* <u>LIFE WITHOUT LIMBS</u>. 09/19/2020. [<u>lifewithoutlimbs.org</u>].

[10] Sterling, Rod. 1959-64. Television Series. *"The TWILIGHT ZONE."* <u>WIKIPEDIA</u>. 09/19/2020. [<u>en.m.wikipedia.com</u>].

[11] Crosby, Fanny. Author. *"To God Be The Glory."* 1875. Words: Public Domain.

[12] Fabarez, Mike. Pastor/Author/Speaker. *"What is the Gospel?"* <u>COMPASS BIBLE CHURCH.</u> YouTube. 09/23/2020. [<u>youtube.com</u>]..

Chapter 8   Precious Pilgrimage

[1] Noah, Ray: Lead Pastor. 2009/06/22. *"PSALM 139: MY DAYS ARE NUMBERED."* <u>Portland Christian Center.</u> Founder. CEO. Petros Network. 10/18/2020. [<u>raynoah.com</u>].

[2] BST & Crosswalk Staff. 2019/08/17. *"15 Amazing Attributes of God: What They Mean and Why They Matter."* <u>Bible Study Tools.</u> 10/20/2020. [<u>biblestudytools.com</u>].

[3] Kaiser, Noelle Parks. Quote used with permission.

Chapter 9   Personal Perspectives From Family & Friends

All personal perspectives have been *used with permission* from each author.

Jet William Zoradi

Calvin Jay Washburn

Eden Joy Zoradi

Millie & The Bible

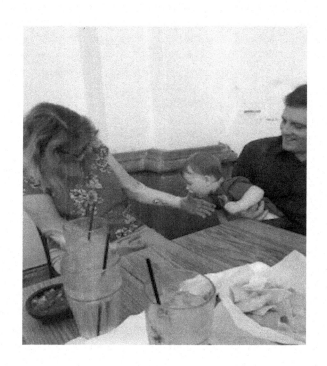

Cal Loves Nana's Hands

Dad Patterson and Vicki at San Clemente Pier

Christmas Day—2019

Christmas Card—2020

SUPPORT—BOOST—CONSIDERATION

*If you enjoyed this book, would you mind helping me out by leaving a review on Amazon?

*How about recommending it to your family, friends, and neighbors?

*Don't forget...Books make awesome gifts as well!

*Please send me your e-mail contact information so I can update you on future books, sale prices, contests, and much, much more.

—Race to Win!

Vicki Zoradi

vickizoradi@gmail.com

Made in USA - North Chelmsford, MA
1208605_9798573655048
12.09.2021 1452